Portland Glass

LEGACY OF A GLASS HOUSE DOWN EAST

Thelma Ladd
&
Laurence Ladd

COLLECTOR BOOKS
A Division of Schroeder Publishing Co., Inc.

Photographs by Laurence A. Ladd

Unless indicated otherwise, all objects are from
the authors' collection.

The current values in this book should be used only as a guide.
They are not intended to set prices, which vary from one section of
the country to another. Auction prices as well as dealer prices vary
greatly and are affected by condition as well as demand. Neither the
Authors nor the Publisher assumes responsibility for any losses that
might be incurred as a result of consulting this guide.

Searching For A Publisher?

We are always looking for knowledgeable people considered to be
experts within their fields. If you feel that there is a real need for a
book on your collectible subject and have a large comprehensive
collection, contact us.

COLLECTOR BOOKS
P.O. Box 3009
Paducah, Kentucky 42002-3009

Additional copies of this book may be ordered from:

The Serena Colby Gallery
P.O. Box 900
York Harbor, ME 03911

or

COLLECTOR BOOKS
P.O. Box 3009
Paducah, Kentucky 42002-3009

@$24.95. Add $2.00 for postage and handling.

Contents

Preface

Time brings change to all things! A painting may slowly change, causing a thin layer of paint that once hid another painting or drawing to become sufficiently transparent to reveal the details beneath it. The effect is called *pentimento*.

Through the years, the quest for the truth about Portland Glass has involved the same kind of process—a scraping away of the myth and hearsay about this little known subject to make time itself transparent, revealing the details obscured by more than a century. *Portland Glass, Legacy of a Glass House Down East* fills a void and adds another facet to the history of Maine.

We have gleaned information about Portland Glass from every corner of Maine and indeed from far afield. It is with the coastal region, however, that we are most concerned, for it was on Casco Bay that the glass house was located. It was also here that the talented people who produced the glass made their homes, as do many of their descendants today.

For those who have never visited this coastline, whose feet have never felt the firm sand of our beaches, who have never tasted the early-morning fog, let me tell you of this enchanted land where the pinelands run greening to the rocky shores and kneel beside the shining sea—a place that through the drifted years has given those it has nurtured a deeper understanding of the mystery of life.

In fair summer, Down East is where the purple lupines blow and the mourning dove nesting in the heart of the spruce forgets to grieve. As twilight gathers and spindrift mists the air, the fog slips silently in from the sea, like a benediction at the end of day, draping the earth in trailing clouds of fleecy white like the graceful hem of His robe.

Everyone who seeks this elusive haven must find his own, for it is a place known only in the heart. No one can ever possess it. Belonging eternally to the great thundering seas that crash against the headlands, it is a land of wind and rain and the loveliness of drifted snow. Since the time of the Red Paint People, this sylvan place by the sea has been home to an industrious and creative society.

We are grateful to those who had the vision to found a glass house in this land of enduring beauty, and we salute the men and women whose artistry produced fascinating Portland Glass. Blessed are they who dream dreams and have the will to make them come true.

Thelma Ladd

Ophidian vase with green serpent; Gone With The Wind lamp signed "P.G. Co."; Nestor berry set in amethyst.

Private Collection

Dedicated To

Franklin Haley Allen

**Bowdin Medical School
Class of 1887**

My Grandfather

Thelma Ladd

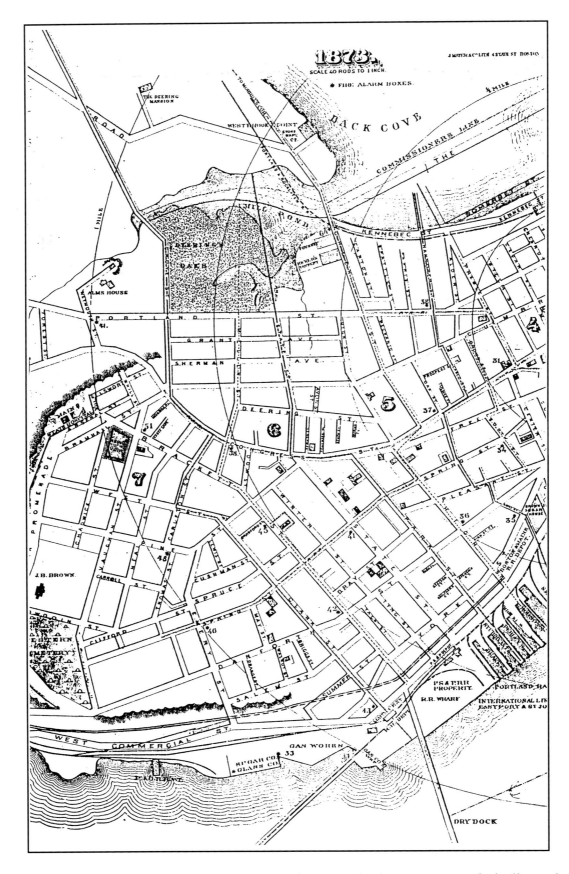

Map of downtown Portland, 1873. Site of Portland Glass Company is indicated by "Glass Co." along the harbor front.

Introduction

Glass has been involved with man—and vice versa—since long before the sun first shone on the pyramids. As far back as 75,000 years before the birth of Christ, Nature's glass, obsidian, abounded. From the earliest times, man used obsidian to fashion spears, arrowheads, and knife blades.

The first man-made glass probably was produced quite by accident during the Neolithic Age when sand and soda were fused in an open fire. The first conscious attempt at glassmaking was no doubt an off-shoot of the potter's art, as it is a natural extension of the glazing process that produced lovely pottery colors. Glazed beads first appeared in Egypt about 12,000 B.C. The earliest-known glass object is a lapis blue amulet dating from 7000 B.C. Fragments of green glass appeared by about 5000 B.C., long before the First Dynasty, and striped glass was in evidence by 3800 B.C. Lovely blue beads were being made by 1570 B.C. Even though many of these early dates are open to question, they certainly indicate that the glassblower's art is an ancient one.

By the time of Egypt's Eighteenth Dynasty (the sixteenth century B.C.), glassmaking had become an established industry. The oldest definitively dated glass object is a large glass bead bearing the cartouche of the Pharaoh Amenhotep (ca. 1551-1527 B.C.) At this point, glass was used almost exclusively for adornment and was considered as precious as Nature's jewels.

As time went on, glass was used to make small hollowware objects, such as small vases. During this early period, the glass was not blown but rather molded, by wrapping thin rods of soft glass around a sand core or by dipping a core in molten glass several times until sufficient thickness accumulated.

The first true molded glass was made in open molds in Egypt about 1200 B.C. This, of course, was the first step on the long path to development of tableware. From then until the Christian era, Egypt remained the glassmaking center of the world.

At about the beginning of the Christian era, the focus of the glassmaking industry shifted to Phoenicia (modern-day Lebanon), where it was advanced immeasurably by the introduction of the blowpipe, the greatest of all glassmaking inventions. Most historians concur that the blowpipe of that era was almost the same as it is today—a tube of iron about four or five feet long with a mouthpiece at one end and a knob at the other end. This device, although simple in concept, opened up the entire field of off-hand blowing and made possible an endless variety of shapes. At about this same time, the first colorless glass was made and termed "crystal," since it was as transparent and as pure as rock crystal.

The method used then—and still used today— is as follows: First the knob end of the blowpipe is dipped into the crucible of hot molten glass. When it is removed, a mass of hot "gather" adheres to the end. By blowing into the pipe while rotating and manipulating it, the glassblower can produce a nearly symmetrical shape. As the mass cools, it is necessary to reheat it from time to time. If the mass is blown into a mold, it will, of course, take on the shape of the mold and become what is known as blown molded glass.

During the early Christian era, the glassmaking industry grew steadily, due in large part to the stabilizing effect of the Roman Empire. Glass manufacture spread throughout the vast empire. Roman glassblowers were highly skilled, and they were masters of nearly all the skills of glassmaking and decorating that are of major importance today. It was during their heyday that one of the world's most famous and beautiful glass vessels was produced. The Portland Vase,* found in the tomb of Alexander Severus, is a beautiful blue vase encased in white with a scene cut through the outer white layer. It later inspired what Josiah Wedgwood considered his finest product, the Jasperware Portland Vase.

After the fall of the Roman Empire, there was a gap of about six centuries from which little information has been gleaned. After the Crusades, the center of the glass industry shifted to Venice, where it remained for the next 400 years. By the year 1292, the industry was well ensconced on the Venetian island of Murano. It is said that there was a full mile of glass houses on the island employing thousands of workers. The factories were located there to eliminate the potential problem of fire in the center of Venice and also to protect the secrets of the glassmaking trade. And protect it they did! No glassmaker was allowed to emigrate, and not even scrap glass could be exported—under penalty of death. By the sixteenth century, the Venetians had perfected the beautiful "cristello," the world's first truly transparent, completely colorless glass. They also produced beautiful colored and decorated glass.

But the secrets of glassmaking could not be protected forever, and it was not long before the famed glass houses of Bohemia began to exert their influence. Glass houses in Germany produced enameled glass. By the eighteenth century, it was being made in France. As early as the sixteenth century, window glass (of poor quality) was being made in England.

It was in England that the modern period of glassmaking began. Because wood was scarce and needed for other uses, the glassmakers were forbidden to burn wood in their furnaces, so they developed a coal-burning furnace that revolutionized the industry. Another major advance that occurred in England was the introduction of flint by George Ravenscroft in 1675. This distinctive glass characteristic was produced by adding lead oxide to the melt to create a softness that facilitated decoration.

It did not take long for glass to reach America. As a matter of fact, the first factory in the New World was a glassworks near Jamestown, Virginia. The first cargo exported from America contained glass. This early factory as well as the second one, built in 1621, lasted only a few years. A longer-lived factory was built in New Amsterdam (New York), where it operated from 1645 to 1767. In 1739, Caspar Wistar established a highly successful factory in southern New Jersey, which was followed by several others. Some of the loveliest glass ever made was produced by Henry William Stiegel at Manheim, Pennsylvania, in a factory that opened in 1765 and closed in 1774, a victim of the depression that preceded the Revolutionary War.

The next high point in the history of American glass was the establishment of the Boston and Sandwich Glass Company in 1825 by Deming Jarves. The company was an instant success, and it flourished until 1887. By 1830, its production had reached 100,000 pounds per week. Jarves obtained several patents, one of which was for the production of glass using iron molds. This launched the production of American pressed glass and led the way to the founding of glassworks in many other areas. Fortunately for the glassmaking tradition, one of these other firms was the Portland Glass Company of Portland, Maine.

*Without a doubt, the Portland vase is the most famous glass vessel of antiquity and the finest example of Greek Cameo Glass. Its name comes from the Duchess of Portland, who gained possession of it in 1780. Later, after her death, the third Duke of Portland lent it to Josiah Wedgwood to copy.

This simple cake stand has no pattern name and was made for the hotel or restaurant trade. The base and standard are identical to those used on some Tree of Life items and provides the means of identification.

Chapter 1

The People and the Place

One of the finest examples of cut glass is this lantern made for C.P. Brackett, watchman at the Portland Glass Company.

Frank H. Swan Collection, Portland Museum of Art, Portland, Maine.

In the year 1863, there was established in Portland, Maine, a company that during its brief career—a mere ten years—produced glass the equal of any made in this country. The Portland Glass Company, under the guidance of Enoch Egginton, was in every respect the equal of the more famous glassworks farther south, but history has been less than kind to the wares of the Portland factory. Little has been written about the firm, and to most collectors its short history remains a fascinating mystery. The pages that follow unveil much of that mystery and put the Portland Glass Company into proper perspective as one of the leading producers of fine glassware in the nineteenth century.

In 1863, glass was made much as it was a thousand years earlier, and, for that matter, much as it is today. The formulas and methods were closely guarded secrets, handed down by each generation just as they were in the famed glassworks on the Venetian island of Murano. The Portland factory was particularly fortunate in having the services of Enoch Egginton, a superlative glassmaker who knew and appreciated the secrets of the art. Not only was Egginton the first superintendent of the glassworks, but he planned and oversaw all the details of the construction of the factory.

From childhood, Enoch Egginton was destined for just such an undertaking. In Bristol, England, where he was born, his father was a master glassblower who trained his son in the art. At an early age, Enoch came to this country and became an American citizen. Before reaching Portland, he worked in Sandwich, Massachusetts, and in the Pittsburgh area. Although lightly built, he was a powerful man who could outperform anyone in the factory. According to the *Eastern Argus* of June 12, 1864, Enoch Egginton could lift a load suitable for a truck horse. He was of nervous temperament, unafraid to soil his hands, and he could be found working in any section of the factory where he was needed. A skilled craftsman, he was able to blow, finish, and cut the most delicate and beautiful glassware.

Not long after the Portland factory opened, Enoch Egginton found that he needed help in the cutting room, so he sent for his younger brother, Joseph, who was then working at the Sandwich Glass Company. Joseph Egginton remained at the Portland factory even after his brother left in 1866 and was foreman of the cutting room as long as the factory was in production. A second brother, Oliver, a glassblower of exceptional talent, also remained to the end. After the closing of the

Portland vaseline candlestick inverts to vase; dark blue Tree of Life sugar.

ortland factory, the three brothers were eunited at the Sandwich Glass Company.

The waterfront factory that Enoch Egginton uilt for owner John Bundy Brown had every modern convenience known to the glass-making world of the time. For example, the Portland plant never had to contend with the problems of a wood-fired furnace. It used coal right from its inception. The coal came from Baltimore on the company's steam bark, the *Arthur Kingman*, unloading its cargo on the company wharf on Portland's waterfront.

The glass furnace used in the original plant was of the conical type (see accompanying diagram).[1] Early furnaces usually were dome-shaped, but the advent of coal created a need to concentrate the heat while allowing the gases to escape freely, so the cone-shaped chimney enclosure was developed. This arrangement allowed the gases to be completely combusted before exiting. The fire was in the central section, with the flames playing around the covered crucibles (huge clay pots) and impinging on the arch above.

The gases produced by the melt, along with the products of the combustion, passed up the conical chimney.

During operation of the furnace, great care was necessary to ensure that none of the venting holes were blocked, which unfortunately occurred on December 6, 1866. A *Portland Transcript* account, dated December 7, tells the story:

EXPLOSION AT THE GLASS WORKS

One of the "glory holes" at the Glass Works exploded Tuesday, shaking the brick work upon which stood the oil tank and injuring eight of the employees, four of them badly but not fatally. One of them, a boy, was taken to the hospital, and the others were well cared for. As the explosion was a gaseous one, it is supposed the vents had become choked so that the gas could not escape. The works were not hindered in manufacture by the accident.

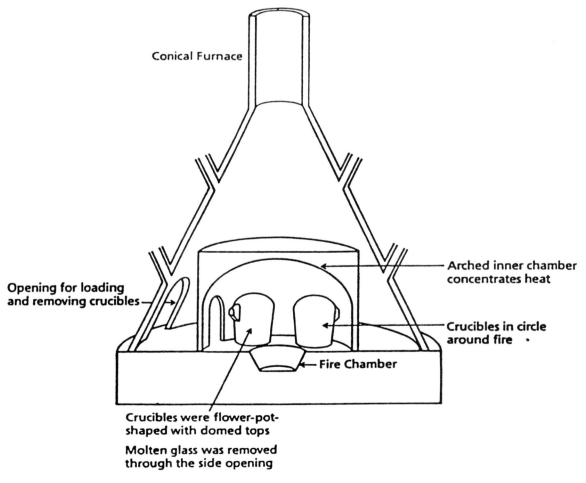

Conical Furnace

Arched inner chamber concentrates heat

Opening for loading and removing crucibles

Crucibles in circle around fire

Fire Chamber

Crucibles were flower-pot-shaped with domed tops

Molten glass was removed through the side opening

Mugs: Garden of Eden, Dahlia, Roman Rosette, Crackle.

This conical type of furnace could, in theory, hold between five and ten crucibles. The one at the Portland factory held eight.[2] The furnace was fifty feet in diameter at the base and seventy feet to the top of the cone. It was constructed of sandstone lined with refractory, or fire, clay.

The crucibles were made of refractory clay from England, since the local clay available in great quantities around Portland was found to be entirely unsuitable. In glassmaking, refractory material must withstand the extreme heat of the furnace without cracking and must be relatively insoluble in the molten glass. (All refractories are to some degree soluble in the melt.) The crucibles were constructed from a mix of about forty percent raw fire clay and sixty percent "grog" (burned fire clay that has been ground and screened). A description of the process that appeared in the *Eastern Argus* on April 16, 1864, is at once vivid and accurate:

> The clay of which the crucible is made is mostly foreign. The English clay is said to be the best and the American the poorest. This clay is ground under a large round stone that rolls in a circular trough, after which it is mixed with clay that has been burned hard and then ground in the mill just mentioned. It is then set out in a large wooden box or pen where it is wet with hot water and trodden with naked feet every day for a number of weeks, before it is in the right condition to be used in the making of pots and crucibles. When the crucibles are dried sufficiently hard to be safely handled, they are lowered from the pot room to the glass house, where they are placed in the immense furnace and kept in a state of red heat for a week before they are filled with the different materials that are here melted into glass.

Unfortunately, the corrosiveness of glass acting on the crucible is such that there was a steady need for new crucibles, and this part of the factory was in constant use. The gradual solution of the clay into the glass melt, of course, affected the quality of the glass produced. A pot with a bottom thickness of five inches when first placed in the furnace would be reduced to only an inch in a few months.[3]

The furnace, which was the "roseleaf" type—meaning that the crucibles were arranged around a central core—held eight pots of 1,700-pound capacity each. The temperature was kept slightly below the melting point of the crucible, even though this greatly increased the strain, because of the obvious advantage in the melting of the glass.

When the mixture that made up the glass

atch was placed in the pot or crucible, the first ingredients to liquefy were the alkali products, which fuse immediately, followed quickly by a reaction with the sand and alkali silicates at about 800 degrees. Lime and other bases then find their complement of silica and enter solution or form double silicates. Excess silica begins to dissolve, the temperature increases, and the melt becomes more fluid. As this is going on, gaseous products are liberated from the carbonates, sulfates, nitrates, and hydrates. The escape of these gases serves to mix the solution thoroughly, as the "cullet" added to the mix does its job of bringing the less soluble materials into solution.

It would seem that as soon as the mixture became fluid, all should be ready for the glass blowing. Not quite! There still remains the necessity of removing the bubbles trapped in the melt. The larger bubbles rise faster due to their greater buoyancy, and, by joining with the smaller bubbles, tend to sweep the mixture clean. The process is best accomplished in a mixture that is heated quickly once it starts to melt. This is why the crucibles and the furnace are brought to very high heat before the glass mix is introduced. If the mix were heated slowly, the large bubbles would be produced and escape early in the process, before the smaller ones had formed, thus leaving the smaller ones in the glass. These small bubbles would escape very slowly, even though the mixture was later heated to a very high temperature. For this reason, much early glass has many small bubbles in it. With Portland Glass, the bubbles that occur are very tiny and more apt to be found in early pieces, since the furnace built after the 1866 fire was of the regenerative type, with more constant temperatures due to the preheating of first one side and then the other by the escaping gases.

Before getting into the fashioning of glassware, this is an appropriate time to step back into the late nineteenth century and take a hypothetical tour of the Portland Glass factory. Over the years, there has been considerable speculation about the glassworks. What did it look like? What exactly went on within its walls? No one today knows! No pictures or even sketches have survived. Unfortunately, the factory existed during the era of the Daguerreotype, which was not used widely for exterior subjects. Nor could newspapers print photos, although it does seem surprising that some enterprising reporter did not at least produce a sketch to publish with the opening day story.

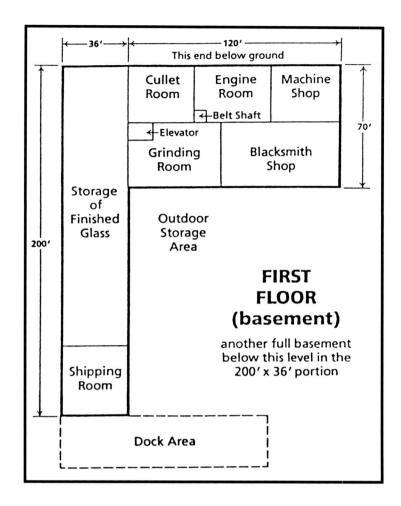

We have done extensive research and even advertised in newspapers over a long period of time, hoping that someone might have a drawing or painting of the factory. Our efforts in that regard have been fruitless, but our research has revealed enough to allow us to produce a descriptive image of the activity in the fascinating brick building on Portland's waterfront. We have pieced this information together bit by bit from many sources, including newspapers of the day, personal interviews with descendants of glassworkers, and a wonderfully enlightening diary of a Maine family. We are grateful for all of these contributions to our knowledge of the operation of the Portland Glass Company.[4]

It is interesting that while this country was

engaged in a civil war, causing a great drain on the economy, a new industry, the Portland Glass Company, came to Maine. As the war neared its end, the citizens of Portland became vitally interested in the round-the-clock activity in the brick building by the bay. What went on within its walls? How were its intricately fashioned products made? Who were the people who accomplished these miracles? Come with us, back in time, and see the wonders of a working glass house Down East.

Just beyond the shovel manufactory on the south side of Canal Street, above the gasworks and adjacent to the Sugar House, stands the substantial four-story brick building—36 feet by 200 feet. An ell, housing the boiler and furnace, measures another 120

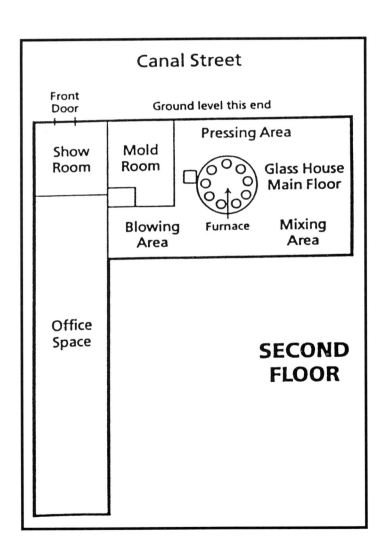

feet by 70 feet. The boiler chimney rises 70 feet, while the furnace chimney reaches a height of 100 feet and belches forth smoke and gases day and night. This imposing edifice is the Portland Glass Company, the enterprise of John Bundy Brown.

As we approach the building, we see piled on the docks the raw materials of the glass produced within, including sparkling white silica from the quartz deposits in Berkshire County, Massachusetts, refractory clay from England, and huge piles of coal to feed the hungry furnace.

Entering the lower floor, we find the packing room, where the glass is prepared for shipment to all parts of the United States.

Portland products are particularly attractive to buyers in the Midwest. The foreman of the packing room is William B. Bent, later to become superintendent of the glassworks.

Close by is the blacksmith shop, with a glowing circular forge where the iron molds and all the other tools of the trade are crafted. The Portland factory is completely self-sufficient, making everything needed right on the premises. The resident mold maker, Dennis Quale, is a genius at taking a clay model and producing an iron mold of great refinement. His brother, Robert, is equally skillful as a blacksmith and also is responsible for all of the brasswork produced at the factory. Together they rule the blacksmith shop, and when it is necessary to hire itinerant moldmakers (such as when a complete set of molds is needed for a new pattern), the brothers watch constantly to be sure that the designs are not stolen before the glass is put into production. (Then, as now, industrial espionage was a fact of life and no amount of watchfulness could prevent mold-makers from spreading design throughout the industry. Without samples however, they were unable to make exact copies, and the first company to start production of a new design was apt to be the most successful with it.)

Also on this lower floor is the engine room housing the twelve-horsepower engine built by Portland's Winslow & Co. A one-cylinder boiler supplies steam for the engine and heats the entire building. Using a complex system of belts, the engine drives all of the factory's machinery. (One early writer described a thunderous noise that erupted when a belt broke and fell three stories from the cutting room to the engine room.)

Next door to the engine room is the cullet room, where the broken glass is sorted and prepared for inclusion in the next batch of glass.

The other room on this floor doesn't have a specific name, but it is one that seems to be most fascinating to the factory's visitors, as descriptions of it appear frequently in newspaper stories. The *Eastern Argus* is one such forum:

> The process of mixing is perfected by operating with the naked feet, which seems to one who stands looking on, as it must be most disagreeable. A sensitive man has a natural horror of putting his feet into the clay in this manner, but the rugged fellows who do the work appear not to care for it, and are cheerful in their employment as they would be if they were working at a duty that was not the least unpleasant. The engine here is one of about twenty horsepower. Whoever has charge of grinding must take heed lest there is danger that he will lose his life. The circular trough which holds the great upright stone is very near the wall of the building. Besides this, the stone passes so close to one of the posts in the room that it almost rubs against the timer. When the clay is ground enough, it is taken out of the trough with a common short-handled shovel, and if the stone were in the wrong position, there would be no way left for him to escape. If one were willing to encourage a careless manner of working, he might suggest that the grinding of clay would be a safer operation if the apparatus could be set in the center of a large room where a man might follow the stone entirely around the trough.

After the grinding operation is complete, the clay is put into a large wooden box or pen, and hot water is added so that the clay can be worked with bare feet. This process takes several weeks, as the clay has to be blended perfectly so that there will be no weak spots in the crucibles.

Varying accounts of the factory put the above facilities either on the first floor or the basement floor. This disagreement seems to come from the fact that one could enter the building on different levels. The street entrance led into the second floor, whereas the dockside entrance led into the first floor, which is what is being described here. (A partial basement was below it.)

From the room just visited, a rope-operated elevator transports the prepared clay to the crucible room on the third floor. For the moment, we will bypass the second floor and go directly to the crucible room. Here are constructed the giant clay pots in which the glass is made. In one corner is a large arched kiln in which the crucibles are fired. The kiln vents directly into the conical chimney of the furnace in the glass house below. The wall adjacent to the kiln is completely open to the glass house, which is two stories high and extends up through the third floor in the center.

Unless flint glass is being made, crucibles traditionally are open. At Portland Glass, all of the crucibles are of the closed type, with a hooded top and a side opening to remove the glass. This prevents the gases and combustion products of the furnace from getting into and discoloring the glass.

When the crucibles have been formed and are dry, they are fired in the kiln and then lowered into the glass house. There they are put into the furnace—not a simple task. To begin with, it is not very easy to handle a pot capable of holding 1,700 pounds of glass. The crucible must be installed in the hot furnace through a fairly small opening, and often it is destined to replace a crucible inconveniently located in the furnace. There already are seven crucibles in there, and they usually are full of molten glass. Once installed in the furnace, the crucible cannot be used until it is brought to full heat over a period of about a week. Often this replacement is the result of a calamity in the form of a crucible that has broken in the furnace, necessitating the removal first of 1,700 pounds of molten glass!

The glass house covers most of the second floor, and this is where glass actually is made. Directly below the crucible room is a room where the molds are cleaned and repaired after use and then stored until needed again. Between this room and the furnace is the area where the materials for the batch are prepared.

This is accomplished by a man with the impressive title of glassmaster. At Portland Glass, this position is held by James Beard, who accompanied Enoch Egginton to the city and acts as his assistant. Like Egginton, he can be found anywhere in the factory where he might be needed. The major job of the glassmaster is to prepare the materials for the melt and to determine the composition of the melt. It is his responsibility to add just the right amounts of chemicals to produce the wondrous colors for which Portland Glass is renowned.

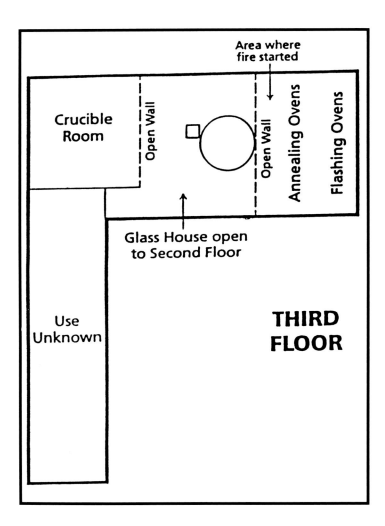

The majority of the glass produced is soda-lime, which is composed of silica in the form of quartz, purified potash, soda in the form of native carbonate, and limestone or lime in the form of crushed marble. This type of glass is distinguished by its low melting point and easy workability. It also is inexpensive and as colorless as the more costly flint glass. The only difference between the formulations of soda-lime and flint glass is the addition o either red or white lead oxides. The exac proportions of these oxides have tremendous effect on the quality of the glas produced—the secret of the art.

The glassmaster's intimate understanding c chemistry is critical to the success of th products; he is in effect a glass chemist because he has to know exactly what trac chemicals to add to produce desired colors Ruby red or pale cranberry, for example comes from the addition of gold chloride Obtaining red requires cooling and reheatin to develop the color. When reheated, tin an silver compounds vary the tint from rose re to a deep red-purple. To produce glass in th yellow-to-brown family, potassium anti monate, silver chloride and silver borate ar added in various amounts. Emerald green i produced with cupric oxide, yellow green wit chromium oxide, and dull bottle green wit ferrous oxide. Blue comes from the addition c cobalt oxide. Shades of blue can be obtaine with the addition of silver chloride an manganese salts. Milk glass is produced b adding bone phosphate, an insoluble whit powder, to the melt. (It could be either flint o soda-lime.)[5]

Near the great furnace are the glass presses where most of the glass is fashioned. A account in the *Portland Transcript*, June 12 1864, explains the activity in this area.

> Two workmen are now engaged in making sugar bowl covers. One of them thrusts an iron rod into the crucible and brings out on the end of it a small mass of glowing melted glass. This he drops into an iron mold fixed in a press. The other workman, with a pair of shears, clips off just enough of the metal to fill the mold—a nice operation requiring skill and practice. He then brings down the level, a follower pushes the melted mass into the mold, and in an instant it is converted into an ornamental article of daily use. This is the method of producing pressed glass ware.

More interesting than pressing to th observer, however, is the process going o across the room, glassblowing, for it is th glassblower who is the true glass artist. I this section of the factory, under the direction of the head glassblower, Robert Robson, we see several men blowing items of great beauty. Each has a small, open furnace for reheating the glass during the blowing process. A glassblower dips a five or six-foot iron tube into the melt and withdraws a blob of glass. By turning the tube while blowing into it, he expands the blob into a globe. While the glass is hot, the artist shapes it with an instrument that resembles a pair of tongs. From time to time the glassblower reheats some or all of the object in order to produce the shape he desires. Working this way, the glassblower can produce almost any imaginable shape. The variety is endless!

The hot glass items are conveyed quickly to the annealing oven on the third floor. Located on the opposite side of the building from the crucible room, it is open on one whole wall to the glass house. The annealing oven is fifty feet long, and it is here that the glass is cooled slowly to eliminate stress in the finished article. The glass is passed through it on iron pans. This portion of the factory is gas-fired. Where the glass enters the oven, it is very hot, with flames waving beautifully over the annealing pans—an awesome sight. As the pans pass deeper into the annealing oven, there is less and less heat, and when the glass emerges at the other end, it has cooled to the point where it can be transported to the fourth floor for the finishing operations.

Just beyond the annealing ovens are the enameling and flashing ovens, also gas-fired. These are used to reheat the glass to a temperature that fuses the enamels and flashing glasses to the glass surface. Then they are annealed again, this time at a much lower temperature.

On the fourth floor, the most delicate processes take place: grinding, etching, polishing, cutting, flashing, enameling, and sandblasting. These finishing procedures are the domain of specialists and require considerable talent and extensive training.

It may seem hard to realize, but two women are responsible for nearly all of the flashing and enameling done at the factory. Judith Mercer, the chief decorator, and Esther Wood, the lamp painter, occupy an area by a large window overlooking the waterfront. One can't help but wonder how they can accomplish anything in this distractingly beautiful spot,

with the great Maine-built ships riding the waves in the harbor below. Many a ship stops at the docks of the Portland Glass Company and picks up a cargo of glass to be traded in the far corners of the world. All around the two women are huge racks of glass just waiting for the finishing touches to turn them into works of art.

Judy Mercer sits with brush in hand carefully decorating a milk glass[6] bowl that may someday journey in the hold of one of those Maine ships. Hers is a painstaking job, requiring application of brightly colored enamels that she creates by grinding special glass that melts at low temperature to a fine powder. Then she mixes the powder with oil of lavender and applies it delicately to the glass with her brush. The object then is reheated to the melting point of the enamel to bond it permanently to the glass surface. The only difference between enameling and flashing is that the enamels are opaque and can be applied thickly to produce a raised decoration, whereas the flashing is transparent enamel applied thinly simply to add color to the glass.

While similar to enameling, the painting of lamps, lamp shades, and lamp chimneys has somewhat different requirements. The materials used are opaque enamels, but they have to be ground much finer, and they are not made at the factory. Most of the enamel paint comes from France and consists of a white or pale-colored powder mixed with oil of lavender. It is applied to the glass or china with a tiny brush. Each color has to be applied separately and then fired before another color is added, and because the colors do not develop until fired it requires a great deal of skill and experience. Portland Glass lamps and painted milk glass reveal great talent in the use of these materials. (This type of enamel was very popular with Victorian-era ladies for painting on both glass and china. All of the beautiful handpainted Limoges china was done in exactly the same way by women at home and then returned to the china shop for firing.)

At the other end of the same fourth-floor room is another big window that illuminates the work of the glass cutters, who have to be incredibly skillful, since even the slightest miscalculation can completely ruin the article in process. Cutting, or engraving,[7] is accomplished with small, rapidly revolving copper disks fed with fine emery and oil. While there certainly are other talented engravers employed at the glass works, without a doubt the finest cutter here is Enoch Egginton.

The acid finishing room is located at the back of the building, behind the cutting section, and it is here that patterns such as Etched Fern, Sebago, Hobnail, and Opaline are finished. The room on the opposite side of the building is used for the rough finishing processes, such as grinding, polishing and sandblasting.

In our tour of the factory, we have missed only a small area of the second floor where the visitor enters from the street side. The first area near this entry is the showroom, where the factory's wares are available for purchase.[8] The walls are pale gray, and the glass is arranged spectacularly on large, round tables draped in black velvet. The room is lighted by large windows with shelves across them. On the shelves is a wide array of Portland Glass, all shimmering in the incoming sunlight. Right by the door is a

table with wonderful blown-glass items for children—brightly colored marbles, ships in bottles, and many other fascinating whimseys. The rest of this part of the building is occupied by office space overlooking the city's docks and waterfront.

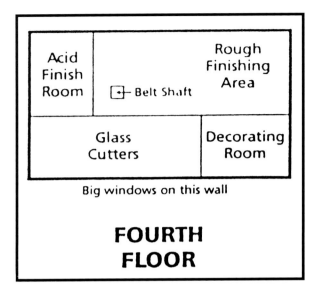

Chapter 2

History of the Portland Glass Company

Blown pitcher made for John Bundy Brown, president of Portland Glass Company.

Collection of Portland Museum of Art, Portland, Maine.

The Portland Glass Company was the dream of one person—John Bundy Brown, a man of widely diversified interests. One of the leading citizens of Portland, he probably did more to help the city prosper than any other person of his era. He was born May 24, 1804, in Lancaster, New Hampshire, the son of a farmer.[1] When he was quite young, he moved to Bartlett (New Hampshire), and later to Gray (Maine), where he met John Smith. The two moved to Portland and took positions as clerks in the wholesale grocery business of Alpheus Shaw who was involved in the East India trade. Eventually Smith and Brown took over Shaw's business, and they continued operating it for many years. Brown's great energy and native ingenuity propelled him into the position of one of Portland's most prominent merchants and manufacturers.

John Brown was active in almost every aspect of Portland's commerce. One of his first big endeavors was the construction and management of the Sugar House, a large sugar refinery on Canal Street, in the waterfront district. He built and operated one of the largest and most elegant hotels in New England, the Falmouth Hotel, and was the major force behind the establishment of the Maine General Hospital. His banking firm, J.B. Brown & Sons, held an enviable international reputation, and he was responsible for the construction of many of the buildings that are Portland landmarks today. When he died January 10, 1881, he left an estate in excess of $4 million.

The Portland Glass Company was formed by a group of the city's leading businessmen, including Charles Jose, Joseph Walker, N. C. Rice, Daniel F. Emery, and of course, the man who first suggested it, J. B. Brown. The first public announcement of the project occurred on April 25, 1863. The site selected was on land owned by Brown adjacent to the sugar factory, a waterfront location that offered advantages for importing raw materials and coal. The first undertaking was the construction of wharves, a proposal that necessitated the following newspaper notice:

> To the commissioners of the Harbor and Tidal Waters of the city of Portland. The undersigned owners of flats and upland in Portland, lying between Vaughn Bridge and the wharf of the Portland Gas Light Co., respectfully represent that they desire to improve the same for wharves and docks; they therefore request that you would fix and establish the wharf line between the above-named points, and also grant to us license to fill and improve the flats within said wharf line.

The petition was approved by the commissioners.

On June 15, 1863, construction began on the brick factory building. By July, the walls were complete and waiting for a roof. The *Portland Transcript* of July 4 indicates that the masonry work was being done by Messrs. Chase and the joinery by Cummings and Brock of Portland. The article stated that glassmaking was expected to begin in late November or early December, and that about 150 persons would be employed initially. It also stated that the company would manufacture all kinds of tableware, kerosene lamps, and more, but no window glass.

Under the expert supervision of Enoch Egginton, the plant was completed a little ahead of schedule, and the first glass made in Maine was produced during the open house

Blown and cut punch bowl made as a presentation piece for Portland Mayor Jacob McLellan (1807-1888). 4⅝"x14¹/₁₆".

Gift of Mrs. Acsah Horne, Portland Museum of Art, Portland, Maine.

on November 12, 1863. Work began at seven that morning in the new glassworks, which boasted the finest physical plant and equipment of any glass company in the world. The factory's workforce on opening day was seventy-eight.

Visitors to the glass factory that first day reported that everything worked admirably and business continued in a lively manner. Guests at the opening were allowed to try their hand at blowing glass, and each received a souvenir in the form of a sauce dish with the Jacob's Ladder pattern. Many of these dishes survive today, although they are of poor-quality green glass with a high bubble content produced prior to opening during equipment tryouts, they are prized by collectors. Opening day also saw the production of a set of thirteen blown glass goblets in Portland Wreath pattern for each of the five directors of the company. The goblet illustrated with the letter S is from one of these sets.

Within a week, the factory was in full production. Mr. Egginton's first order of business, according to the family diary, was to complete a set of stemware for Mrs. Abraham Lincoln at a cost of $4,000. This commission was directed to Enoch Egginton personally, not to the company.[2]

The Portland Glass Company was incorporated in January 1864 by a special act of the Maine Legislature, which was signed by Governor Samuel Cony February 4, 1864. The capital stock authorized by the Legislature was $75,000, and the factory was granted a five year exemption from all taxes. The president and principal stockholder of the corporation was John Bundy Brown and the treasurer was J.S. Palmer. The board of directors was an illustrious one, consisting of Rensellaer Cram (who was also a director of the Portland Company, treasurer of Westbrook Manufacturing, president of the Portland Rolling Mills, president of Merchants National Bank, and director of the Portland and Ogdensburg Railroad), Joseph Walker, Charles E. Jose (a Portland merchant), and George Brock (the contractor). These gentlemen held the same positions throughout the entire life of the original company.

Before long, orders were arriving at the

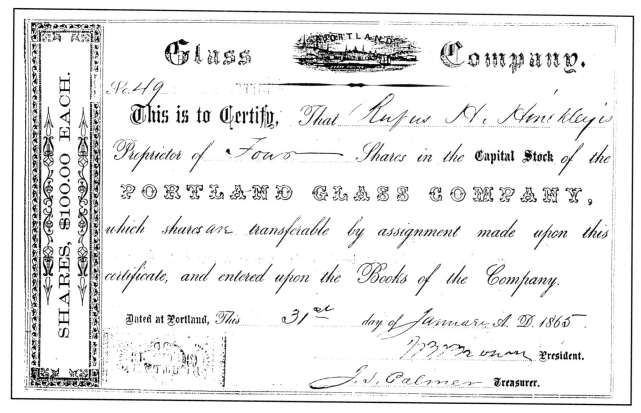

Stock certificate, Portland Glass Company, 1865.

Collection of Portland Museum of Art, Portland, Maine.

Portland Glass factory much faster than they could be filled. Much of the early production was sold right in Portland by Charles Jose, who owned a store on Fore Street that dealt primarily in glass, china, and britannia. By the end of January 1864, the daily production at the factory had reached five thousand articles of glass, and more than a hundred persons were employed there.

It soon became obvious that the facility had to be expanded, and at the January 1865 meeting of the board of directors, the capital stock was increased to $100,000. The stockholders as of that date were John B. Brown, St. John Smith, Horatio Jose, Thomas R. Jones, Rensellaer Cram, J.S. Palmer, Leonard Billings, Joseph Walker, George Brock, Sewall Chase, Charles Jose, and Enoch Egginton. Egginton's shares were given to him as an inducement to remain in Portland even though his original contract had expired.

By October 1865, the addition was nearly finished, including the installation of a new regenerative-type furnace with a capacity of twelve crucibles. The plan was to use the new furnace for the production of ordinary pressed glass. The original, smaller furnace was to be used for the fancy glassware and blown products, including all of the flint glass production. Enoch Egginton had agreed to remain until the new facility had been put into service.

In November, fire—the nemesis of all glass factories—struck the Portland facility for the first time when a pot of molten glass burst. The glass overflowed the furnace and ran down to the floor below, where it ignited a pile of coal. The Portland Fire Department arrived and quickly extinguished the fire, averting calamity. Damage, under $500, was covered by insurance, and production continued without interruption. Total production for that year exceeded a million items, and the board of directors declared a dividend of seven percent.

By early 1866, the new addition was in full

Blown wheel–cut glass, engraved "V.C.A. & P.C. to C.C.T." (Initials stand for Venerable Cunner Association & Propeller Club to Charles Cook Tolman)
Collection of Portland Museum of Art, Portland, Maine.

operation, and, as agreed, Enoch Egginton left Portland. This proved to be a greater loss than had been imagined, because his replacement, James Beard, the expert former glassmaster, was not equal to the new position, and the factory's quality and efficiency suffered greatly.

For whatever reason, the Fourth of July was celebrated with great fervor in 1866. There were cannons, bells, and an impressive parade complete with military detachments, fire equipment, marching civic groups, floats, and several bands. In the part of Portland then called Deering Pasture was a circus with a big top, and the delayed arrival of a giant balloon was anxiously awaited. The Portland Glass Company had even created a new commemorative pattern showing a balloon. Continuing efforts to locate authentic examples of this pattern have been fruitless. (It may be the pattern known as Balloon, but there is no proof.) The tiny blown-glass novelties for children in the form of balloons that the company also made for the occasion have been equally elusive. All of this activity and excitement attracted crowds of visitors from all the surrounding communities.

About four o'clock in the afternoon, the alarm was sounded for a fire in a shipbuilding facility on Commercial Street, near Maple Street. The same wind that had prevented the giant balloon from reaching Portland was still blowing strongly, and the fire soon spread to the wooden houses on Fore Street. The fire department was unable to reach the blaze from either Commercial Street or Fore Street because of the wind, and soon flaming debris reached Brown's Sugar House, which was surrounded by wood destined for the cooperage that made the barrels for the sugar and glass. The wood was quickly engulfed in flames, and the fire soon was well beyond the control of the few steam engines supplemented by hand tubs. The meager water supply was exhausted.

Almost all of the buildings in the fire's path were wood, and the draft created by the blaze only added to the ferocity of the wind, which swept the fire throughout the city. The whole area seemed to explode with a shower of burning debris that resembled nothing so much as a volcano. As the fire tore through the city, buildings collapsed with thunderous roars. Brick, stone, and wood all fell to the power of the great conflagration. Even the iron rails of the trolley tracks on Middle Street were twisted like strands of spaghetti. Furniture dragged frantically from houses simply burned up in the streets. As night approached, the sky looked like a giant scarlet canopy.

Firefighters were helpless in battling the inferno. The only hope for stopping it was to create a firebreak by demolishing buildings with explosives. The fire burned through the night, destroying everything in its path from Commercial Street to Back Cove, on the other side of the peninsula. When daylight broke, the extent of the devastation became evident. The old wooden observatory, high on Munjoy Hill, had been spared, and from it one could look out over the blackened city. Gone were the Custom House, the Post Office, the new City Hall, eight hotels (including Wood's Marble Hotel, just nearing completion), all the newspaper offices, every bank, nearly all of the offices and retail stores. More than 1,800 buildings were destroyed, making this the largest disaster the United States had experienced.[3] But off in the distance, rising proudly from the ruins, stood the great Sugar House and the glassworks of J.B. Brown!

As help poured in from all over the country, the determined people of Portland set out to rebuild their city, using brick as their primary construction material. No fire, even one of this magnitude, could destroy Portland, a city rich in history and tradition. The 11,000 homeless were housed in quickly constructed barracks, but one of the biggest problems arose from the fact that very little insurance could be collected. Since most insurance was handled by local underwriters whose records were destroyed in the fire, there was little that could be done. The few businesses that survived hired extra personnel to try to save the economy of the city. The Portland Glass company was a great boon.

At the annual board meeting of the Portland Glass Company in January 1867, the directors raised the capital stock to $150,000 and declared a seven percent dividend. During 1866, more than 976,000 pieces of glass were produced, including 40,000 dozen kerosene lamps (and lamp chimneys) and 100,000 whiskey and wine glasses. The company by this time had several sales offices and showrooms in such cities as Boston, New York, Chicago, and Philadelphia.

The directors of the corporation recognized

the fact that the reputation of the company was suffering from poor management, and they determined to return it to its former status by hiring a new superintendent. The man selected was William O. Davis, one of the best-known and most respected glassmakers of the time. He had previously been employed at the O'Hara Glass Works in Pittsburgh, where he had invented a revolutionary new glass press. Since Davis owned the patent on it, Portland Glass was able to upgrade its presses, making it possible to nearly double the plant's output. Not only was Davis superb in the technical field of glassmaking, but he also was a designer of glassware, and he put this expertise to immediate use when he arrived at Portland Glass.

During this period, the famed Tree of Life pattern was created, causing a great stir in the glass industry. It was an immediate success and was, more than any other factor, responsible for the rapid recovery of Portland's prestige. This was one of only three designs

for which patents were obtained by the company. On May 22, 1869, Davis received a second patent for Loop and Jewel With Round Ornaments. Like Tree of Life, this was a very successful pattern; production on it had started in 1868, well before the patent was granted. The Patent Office was extremely slow, and patents were evaded easily. Thus, both patterns were copied by other factories with minor changes but with much less success.

It was not long after the arrival of William O. Davis that disaster struck the Portland factory.[4] Just after 10 p.m. on September 18, 1867, the fire alarm was sounded to summon firefighters to the glassworks. The fire was discovered almost simultaneously by C.P. Brackett, the glassworks nightwatchman, and the nightwatchman at the Sugar House. The Sugar House's pumps were put to use quickly under the orders of that company's superintendent, a Mr. Meyers. Five streams of water were directed into the main building. When the Portland Fire Department arrived,

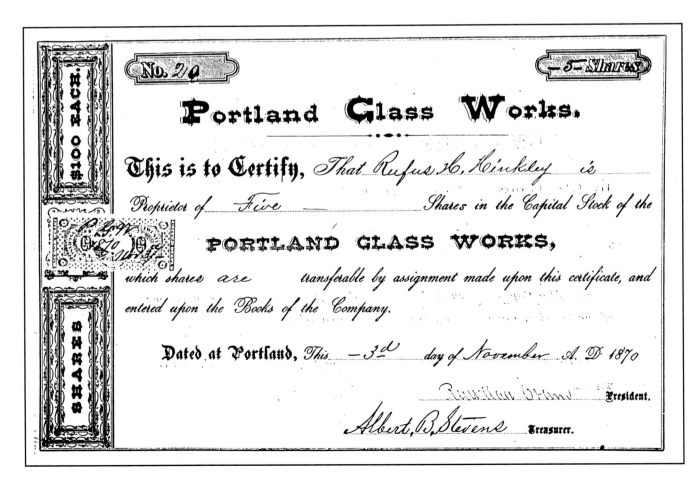

Stock certificate, Portland Glass Works, 1870.

Collection of Portland Museum of Art.

he refinery people turned their attention to wetting down all the combustibles in the area. The fire spread so quickly that the city's steam pumps were unable to contain it. When morning arrived, all that was left of the main building were the walls and the furnace. Incredibly, the addition with the new furnace was untouched.

Somehow, workmen were able to remove most of the finished glass from the building. Insurance covered only about half of the $100,000 loss, but it was a boon that neither furnace was damaged, nor was the crucible room with its new crucibles. Unfortunately, most of the molds were lost.

The fire began in the annealing oven and quickly spread to the carpentry shop above it, where it was first discovered. The company had recently purchased two fire annihilators, which were kept by the nightwatchman but were never put into use. If they had been, perhaps the fire could have been brought under control.

The directors decided unanimously to rebuild immediately. The company resumed limited production in the undamaged addition within three weeks, and reconstruction was complete in six months, when the factory was operating at full capacity. Amazing as it may seem, the total production for 1867 was substantially greater than that of the previous year. Orders were still way ahead of production and there was no interruption in payment of dividends to stockholders.

For awhile, everything went smoothly. Production was at an all-time high level, as was the quality. Orders still exceeded production and stockholders received their dividends. Little information is available for this period except for odd items, such as the fact that the employes presented a harness and buffalo robe to William O. Davis at Christmas in 1869.

Early in 1870, the Portland Glass Company was hit with several strikes by workers. In August of that year it became necessary to reorganize the company, and on August 29 the Portland Glass Company ceased to exist. In its stead was a new company, The Portland Glass Works, with capital of $72,000 and forty-two shareholders, many of them former creditors of the old company. (See Appendix III for complete list.) John Bundy Brown turned his interest over to his son Philip. The new board

of directors consisted of Rensellaer Cram, Philip H. Brown, John Donnell, A.K. Shurtleff, C.E. Jose, Charles S. Forbes, and James H. Smith. Cram was designated president.

A few months later, misfortune struck again. The company steamship, the *Arthur Kingman*, bound from Baltimore to Portland with 594 tons of coal, sprang a leak in a storm off Nantucket and went down. The captain and crew were picked up by a pilot boat. After this loss, the company had to pay to have coal shipped to Portland, adding greatly to the expense of making glass. The fortunes of the factory continued to decline.

In May of 1871, production was suspended because of an oversupply of finished glass, and the factory did not reopen until September 19. By the following May, one furnace was being used, and the wares found a good market. In August 1872, the board of directors selected Rensellaer Cram to continue as president, and he served until his death the following December. His successor was James H. Smith.

In 1873, a nationwide panic caused many healthy companies to close their doors. In August of that year, William O. Davis left the Portland Glass Works to return to Pittsburgh and work for Duncan Glass. His replacement was William B. Bent, whose job was not to make glass but to dispose of existing inventory and assets, including molds and patents. The great furnaces had made their last glass. By the end of 1873, the premises were vacated, and a year later were taken over by Manning Bros., a firm engaged in the production of terra alba. The Portland Glass Works assets that had not been disposed of were sold at auction by F.O. Bailey Company on June 8, 1881. The waterfront property was sold to H.N. Jose for $26,500. That July, bondholders received partial payment on the mortgage.

The failure of this well-respected glassmaking firm had four contributing causes: labor disputes, the increased cost of transporting coal, increased competition from factories closer to the sources of supply, and the general malaise of the national economy.

Ten years seems like a short life for a corporation, yet it is not at all short when measured by the standards of other glassworks of the era. Fortunately, this company was prolific, so that after more than a century, collectors still find splendid examples of the firm's wares. In 1873, the closing of a glass factory had no more significance than the closing of a shoe factory today. There was no one interested in preserving the memory of this fine glassworks. As time went on, the memory faded, and only a few interested people with some family connection to the factory managed to preserve small bits of its history.

By the turn of the century, the heyday of the glass industry had come to an end, and the finest nineteenth-century glass houses were history. But it was not long before collecting became popular and interest in the history of American glass spurred research into the subject. Unfortunately, by this time it was a little late, and information that once was readily available took painstaking research to uncover. Books on American glass published at this time barely hinted at the one-time existence of a fabulous glass house Down East.

If Frank Swan, a Providence, Rhode Island newspaperman, had not needed a birthday present for his wife in the 1930's, this sad situation might never have been reversed. As fate would have it, Swan stopped to look for a gift in an antiques shop on his way home one day. One of the items he considered buying was a goblet with a pattern like the skin of a melon. When the dealer told him it was Portland's Tree of Life, he bought it, but only because both he and his wife were originally from Portland. She liked the piece and suggested that they try to find more to make a set of six. This proved no easy task, and it launched the Swans into a major collecting effort that resulted in the publication of two limited-edition books on Portland Glass.

When Frank Swan died in 1956, his collection was the largest in existence and contained many one-of-a-kind pieces. It was bequeathed to the Portland Museum of Art, forming the basis of its glass collection. From time to time, the museum has acquired additional examples, and today it has the finest collection of Portland Glass in existence—and all because Frank Swan needed to buy his wife a birthday present.

(Note: Although small quantities of Frank Herbert Swan's books on Portland Glass were printed, and copies are hard to locate, it is sometimes possible to find them in used bookstores, particularly in New England. *Portland Glass Company* was published by Roger Williams Press in Providence, Rhode Island, in 1939, and *Portland Glass* was published by the same press in 1949. Swan wrote one other book, *Warren Phillips Lodge 1882-1902* (Westbrook Gazette Printing, 1902).

Chapter 3

The Story of a Town
Lost Deep in the Woods

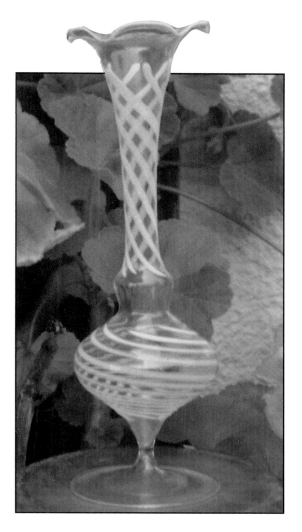

The most recent addition to the author's collection is this exquisite vase blown by Oliver Egginton. Note that the lattice design is white and very pale blue. This and another vase and the blown-glass ewer (shown on page 33) are the only known pieces of this type made at Portland. Without a doubt many other specialty items were made there, but positive attribution can be extremely difficult. Reliable identification of this vase was possible only because it is identical to one owned by a family with ties to the Portland factory.

Private Collection

A few years ago, collectors of Portland Glass heard rumors about an old barn in the wilderness harboring a great treasure—unopened barrels of Portland Glass packed just as it was shipped from the factory. Rumor is like a fire; it feeds itself on the telling. Eventually the rumor appeared in print,[1] alleging that there were several barrels of Portland Glass on a farm in the Damariscotta region. Barrels did indeed exist there, but when they were opened, they contained a mixture of Portland and other glass that had been removed from an antiques shop that had closed a few years earlier. The barrels had no connection with the Portland factory. The rumor was laid to rest—or so it seemed.

The rumor continued to resurface occasionally among collectors, and a few years later, we received a letter from that well-known person, Mr. Anonymous.[2] The letter pinpointed the location of the now-famous barn. Looking at maps, we realized that the site was in now almost uninhabited country. We contacted a friend who often went hunting in the area, and he told us that it was almost impossible to reach, since it was deep in the wilderness. He went on to explain that there was an old logging road into the area, but that it was impassable because of washouts and blowdowns. He cautioned us not to attempt the trek with our car.

Several weeks later, our hunter friend called and suggested laughingly that we go on a safari into Maine's wilderness. The party was assembled. Five of us would go in two Jeeps. The day our friend arrived to pick us up, we realized what an experienced woodsman he was. One of the Jeeps was loaded with food, water, extra clothing, all sorts of camping equipment, and even towing chains. He was prepared for anything and everything.

It was a day's trip just to the beginning of the old logging road, where we stayed that first night. The next morning, as we prepared to embark on the real adventure, we asked our friends if they were convinced we might find the legendary Norumbega at the end of the trail. Each was confident that we would—perhaps just as confident as the early explorers of Maine who had hoped to find that fabled spot.

The first couple miles were not too difficult, but after that, we entered a different world. Our progress often was hampered by fallen trees that had to be cleared. We camped ou that night and by late the next afternoon, we arrived at the lost town.

The scene was like something from the imagination of Edgar Rice Burroughs. The memory of it still haunts us. Doors of modes homes hung open, and everywhere there was a look of desolation. There were little patches o gone-to-the-wild gardens, and, now and then the eye caught the gleam of asters in the sun Lilac bushes by doorways grew tall and wild The remnants of a broom by the front stairs o a cottage made us wonder whose hands had held it so very long ago. A faded gray rope hammock between two trees swung in the warm autumn breeze. The wind seemed to whisper as it came from everywhere and nowhere.

Inside the buildings, it looked as though the inhabitants had just walked out and left everything suspended in time. In some cottages, dishes still remained on the tables Old cupboards were filled with wonderful bric-a-brac, but there were many indications o vandalism. One house contained a beautifu brass bed that sparked a gleam in the eye o one of our companions. Who lived here? Why did they leave? Where did they go? A few letters strewn around were unenlightening.

Around the bend of the sandy road stood a weather-beaten gray barn leaning away from the prevailing wind. Yes, the barrels were inside! They remained just as they had left the factory, destined for the town's only store. The return address was clearly visible: P.G. Co., Portland, Maine.

As we watched and waited with mounting tension, squeaky sounds accompanied the removal of the rusty nails from the barrels. Inside was glass that had not been seen for a century. Here were samples of patterns that had been in doubt, and were now completely confirmed! The temptation was great, but the glass even though long abandoned, did not belong to us.* So we made a complete inventory of the treasure (see Appendix IV) and then repacked it carefully in the sawdust and recovered the barrels for a future generation to find.

None of us wanted to stay in the town overnight—it belonged forever to the past—and so, as dusk approached, we left to return to our campsite. Before leaving, however, we fastened the gaping doors on the houses. That seemed like the only kindly gesture we could make.

Since our journey into the wilderness, we have tried to learn the history of this abandoned town, one of many such places in New England. Apparently at one time there was a mill nearby in which all of the townspeople worked. When it burned down, everyone just left, taking only personal belongings. As in so many other mill towns, all of the property would have been rented from the mill.

Although we acquired no treasure there, we did have a memorable adventure. Each year when Indian Summer explodes in a last burst of glory, we think of that little abandoned town deep in the woods and wonder whether the strange wind still whispers through the vacant windows and sagging doors in the homes where footsteps are heard no more. For years we planned to return there, but now we have decided that it is best to consider it only as a memory. We like to imagine the long-lost barrels still standing there in the old gray barn.

Flow-Blue cup plate from "the lost town."

*Walking back up the road in the late afternoon sun, we found a little Flow-Blue cup plate almost buried in the sand. Perhaps because it had been abandoned to the earth, I felt I could remove it, and with joy slipped it into my sweater pocket. Another member of our group was overjoyed to find a Poland Spring Moses bottle that had been tossed in the bushes.

Thelma

Chapter 4

Is It Really Portland?

Frosted Leaf lamp with milk glass base.
Frank H. Swan Collection
Portland Museum of Art, Portland, Maine.

In the realm of antiques, it is unwise to try to be too positive about anything. All too many experts have fallen into the trap of saying that a certain pattern was produced only by one company, or was made at a specific time because it resembled another pattern made at that time.

We cannot be absolutely certain that any Portland pattern was made only at Portland Glass Company. When we say that a design was not made elsewhere, what we mean in such a case is that we can find no other attribution. When we say that a design originated at Portland, we are making that assumption based on the fact that we have found no evidence that it was previously produced elsewhere.

We can say with complete confidence that every pattern covered in this book was made by the Portland Glass Company. We have confirmed each pattern to our complete satisfaction, except for the one known as Orbed Feet. Even though we have been unable to confirm it, we have included it because it was identified by Frank Swan, who was correct in all of his other identifications, and because we find no indication to the contrary. It is a relatively minor pattern and not at all common, so our inability to make an independent confirmation is not surprising.

The best way to confirm identification is to find a piece of glass with a complete provenance going right back to the factory. Of course, a design patent is strong evidence that the pattern originated at the factory, but it is not indisputable. In that pre-computer era, the Patent Office could not possibly double-check every application to see whether a company already was making the product or whether it had been made in the past. Therefore, there was nothing to prevent other companies from subsequently using Portland Glass patterns or even patenting them. Many writers have alleged—basing their assertions on patent applications or catalogs—that both the Shell and Tassel design and the Shell and Jewel design originated long after the closing of the Portland factory. These assertions are wrong. Both of these patterns were made at Portland prior to the later versions.

When the Portland factory closed, the molds were sold and the buyers proceeded to make use of them. We know, for example, that the Tree of Life and the Loop and Jewel designs both were made at Sandwich. There is no question that Feather was made by the Indiana Glass Company, probably in Portland's molds. There has been some speculation about the slight variations in the Feather design, but apparently changes were made in the design at Portland, thus making it impossible to distinguish between the products of the two factories.

Even when a design was first introduced, other factories were quick to copy successful patterns. As mentioned earlier, there was no way to stop this practice, since itinerant moldmakers carried designs from one factory to another, often before the originator could begin production. With more than 150 glass factories in the United States at the time of the establishment of the Portland Glass Company, it is easy to understand why competition for skilled craftsmen was keen. Each time they moved from one job to another, patterns traveled with them. Certainly when William O. Davis arrived in Portland from the O'Hara Glass Works, he brought along ideas and patterns, just as he took Shell and Tassel to his new employer, the Duncan Glass Company, when he left Portland.

Although experience provides a "feel" for the glass produced by a certain company, it is impossible to determine the origin of an individual piece of glass with any degree of accuracy. Sometimes gross differences in the glass make it possible to assert that a piece of glass probably is not the product of a certain factory, but slight differences were manifest in every batch of glass at every factory. Thus, an expert can specify which items were likely to have been produced at the Portland factory, but there always will be some doubt. In fact, there are some patterns, such as Oak Leaf Band and Oak Leaf Medallion, that we can only assume were made exclusively at Portland because of their scarcity and the fact that they are seldom found beyond the area.

Collectors of Portland Glass are fortunate in that they do not have to be greatly concerned about reproductions. Birch Leaf sauce dishes have been reproduced and sold in huge quantities, but only in clear glass of definitely inferior quality. The Owl and Possum goblet has been reproduced, but the copy has a straight stem instead of the slightly crooked stem of the original. The Loop and Jewel sauce dish was badly reproduced, with poor stippling and rough edges.

In addition to the above reproductions, which were made about forty years ago and are now becoming collectible themselves, there is a new generation of reproductions, which are more easily identifiable, since they are clearly marked. A reproduction of Magnet and Grape, for example, has an MMA signature on it. The glass is of excellent quality, as is the glass in the Broken Column reproduction, which is clearly marked SI in block letters.

Other patterns we have seen that have been reproduced in recent years (all are marked) include Fine Cut and Block, Greek Key, Frosted Leaf, and Roman Rosette. The seem to be no colored reproductions exce Fine Cut and Block, in blood red and hideous shade of bright green. The glass these reproductions is substantially heavi than the originals.

As time passes, it becomes increasing difficult to confirm the origins of pattern There are fewer and fewer people wł remember the history of family heirlooms. our mobile society, many families (and the glassware) have moved away from th Portland area, and contact has been lost. the future, investigators are likely to be eve less successful than we have been, since tł advancing years continue to make the tas more complex.

Chapter 5

Blown-Glass & Novelties

Very delicate blown-glass ewer.

Frank H. Swan Collection,
Portland Museum of Art, Portland, Maine.

The pressed-glass products of the Portland Glass Company have always been its best-known items. Little of the firm's reputation has been based on blown-glass products, even though both types probably were nearly equal in volume of production. This is due primarily to a lack of identification of blown items. As more and more of the blown-glass has been identified, the outstanding quality and craftsmanship of Portland's blown-glass has been recognized.

As with Portland's pressed products, most of the blown items were not fine glass. Lamp chimneys represented nearly half of the blown-glass production, as they were made in huge numbers. Many lamp bases were made of blown-glass, but almost all of these remain unidentified.

Occasionally, an item will appear to be one of Portland's unique patterns, and close examination will reveal that it is blown-glass made in a pressed-glass mold. For example, a charming blue Waterford (Sunburst) witch ball was blown into a cruet mold and removed while hot and expanded into a ball.

A great deal of delicate and lovely stemware certainly was made, but it remains unrecognized. More than likely, all of the forms that were used for cutting were also available plain. Unfortunately, unless plain items can be matched with known decorated ones—or traced to the factory—there is no means of identification. Even many of the decorated forms are not known.

At the Portland Glass Company, there was an elderly glassblower named Emmit Drake, who worked in a dark corner near the annealing oven.[1] Drake worked only on items meant for the amusement of children! Even today's sophisticated children would be enthralled by his wondrous creations. Of course, he also made simple items such as beautiful colored marbles that today are a collector's delight. In those days, a youth could buy a whole bag full at the company showroom for just a few cents. Drake's lovely paperweights, which at the time were considered ordinary and practical, today are extremely rare and valuable.

These ordinary items that could have been made at almost any glass company were not Drake's real claim to fame. His particularly wonderful items were toys of marvelous intricacy. One of these, made for the American Museum of Natural History in New York, is a replica of a fully rigged Kennebec River sailing

Portland Glass marbles.

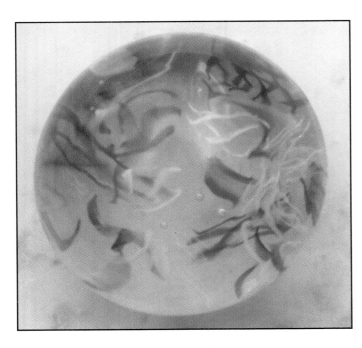

Paperweight.

Paperweight.

ship in a bottle two feet in diameter! When the bottle was empty, the ship sat folded up on the bottom, but when the bottle was filled with water, the ship unfolded and sailed majestically on the water's surface, proudly flying a red, white, and blue flag. Although this masterpiece was unique, many children had some of his smaller ships in bottles. Drake's imagination seems to have been unbounded.

Portland Glass was not famous as a producer of bottles, but the factory did produce some. The American Museum of Natural History commissioned a large set of specimen bottles in myriad sizes with ground-glass stoppers. The largest bottle in the set was said to be the largest blown bottle known at the time. It was three feet high and measured two feet in diameter. It was a perfect cylinder, as were all the other bottles in the set. Quite an accomplishment for a company not known for its bottles.

Many other types of blown-glass items certainly were made at the Portland factory, but many have gone unrecognized. For example, no one would have dreamed that the beautiful blown-glass turquoise ewer owned by the Portland Museum of Art was a Portland Glass product if its origin had not been known. We recently purchased, from the grand-daughter of the blower, a blue and white vase of very similar design that has also been traced to the factory.

Ophidian paperweight.

Witch Balls and Wizards' Sticks

When the subject of witch balls is raised, the usual response is astonishment or amusement, followed by the question, "What are they?" For collectors of old glass, they are a delightful expression of the glassblower's art.

The witch ball originated long ago in Europe as a small, spherical bottle filled with holy water. Later, clear balls were silvered on the inside so that a witch, upon seeing her own image, would be frightened away. The earliest examples of intricate and handsome blown-glass balls were made at the Nailsea Glassworks in England around 1820. They boasted beautiful loopings of colored glass.

The earliest American witch balls were made of clear or green glass and date from 1739 to 1780,[2] products of the first glass house of importance, the Wistar Glass Company in southern New Jersey. Later, all of the New England glass firms made them, as did other plants in New Jersey and Pittsburgh.

During that dark period of our history, when belief in witches was rampant, witch balls protected many a New England home. They were filled with herbs and hung from attic rafters or stood in elegant holders on living-room mantels. Some were suspended in windows or over doorways. Even farm animals were protected by these charming whimseys, and fine examples sometimes are found hanging in old barns.

Even experts who recognize witch balls often have difficulty identifying them. A witch ball always has an opening where a pontil was broken off. Sometimes that opening was enlarged so that herbs could be placed inside to enhance the protective value. The diameter of a witch ball ranges from two inches to fourteen inches, and the glass often is quite thick, particularly in older specimens.

There are also blown-glass balls that were made for other uses. Some were used as stoppers for bowls or pitchers (Portland Glass made some examples of them), but these were always completely closed, as were the balls made for use as fish net floats. Target balls for trapshooting were small—one to three inches, with a half-inch opening—and were made of rather thin glass. Early specimens were plain colored, but later versions were decorated with animals, hunting scenes, or even advertisements.

The most beautiful witch balls were made in the nineteenth century by the New England glass companies. The balls had loopings of color much like those produced at Nailsea. In our collection are two of the finest examples of this type made at the Portland Glass Company by glassblower John H. O'Brien. Of cranberry glass with different-patterned loopings of milk-white glass, they occupy a special niche in our collection because of their origin.

Cobalt witch ball with large hole for herbs.

One lovely summer afternoon, a charming woman from Portland arrived at our gallery gingerly carrying something wrapped in a towel. After spending some time viewing our glass collection, she told us that she had brought along a family heirloom. When she unfolded the towel, we gasped in delight at the sight of two magnificent witch balls. John O'Brien had fashioned them for her Aunt Elizabeth, perhaps as a wedding present. But, sad to say, Elizabeth died before marrying—at the age of twenty-two. The witch balls remained in the family and occupied a place of honor on the mantel. Unfortunately, their delicate vaselike holders

had been broken when our visitor was a child. She now wanted the witch balls to be passed on to someone who would appreciate their historic value.[3] We must have met with her approval, because they are now in our collection. Over the years we have owned other Portland Glass witch balls, but never any as lovely as these.

At Portland Glass, witch balls were made in solid colors such as cobalt, amber and green, as well as with varying looped patterns in blends of cranberry, white, blue, and clear glass. Their sizes ranged between three and six inches. These pretty baubles have become very expensive, and the finest examples can easily bring thousands of dollars.

The witch balls must have been very popular, for only one witch (in this case a wizard) is reported to have lived east of the Piscataqua River, and that was long before the establishment of the Portland Glass Company. George Burroughs, who preached in Falmouth from 1685 to 1690, was tried and convicted of being a wizard in Salem, Massachusetts.[4] There never was a prosecution for the crime of wizardry in Maine.

Balls were not the only glass objects used to ward off witches and wizards. Witches' sticks (also called wizards' sticks) were used for the same purpose. By the time they were made at Portland Glass, however, they were no longer used to ward off evil. They were simply highly ornamental glass canes used in the theater and for such ceremonial purposes as parades. Our collection includes an exceptional spiraling stripe cane that matches our cranberry and white witch balls. Wizards' sticks (or canes) were made at most of the New England glass houses, but none are finer than those produced at the Portland Glass Company.

Pair of cranberry and white witch balls and wizards' stick.

Chapter 6

Specialty Items: Lamps and Salts

Gone With The Wind lamps, signed "P.G. Co." on brass base. These show the superb brasswork of Robert Quale.

The lamp on the left is from a private collection.

Throughout the time that the Portland Glass Company was in operation, the demand for oil lamps was prodigious, since they provided the principal source of illumination throughout the country. Gas was available in major population centers, but not elsewhere. Thus, lamps were the biggest part of the production of any glassworks.

At Portland Glass, the selection of oil lamps was large. It included very simple lamps as well as more elaborate types. At the bottom of the list is a simple patented lamp with a clear glass font on a high, clear standard, with an applied handle on the standard. This lamp has a simple elegance that could be dressed up with one of the company's fancy painted chimneys.

Blown-glass lamps were made in many shapes and sizes—in clear as well as in most colors. Among the colors were amber, light blue, green, and ruby. It is impossible to confirm the identity of the blown lamps unless the complete provenance is known—which creates a problem for the collector. Occasionally, the blown lamps were made with cut patterns that sometimes can be matched to known cutting patterns, thus making identification more accurate.

In this same category are hand lanterns on which the glass was blown and often etched or cut with distinctive patterns. A particularly lovely example, now part of the Swan collection at the Portland Museum of Art, was made for C.P. Brackett, the watchman at the glassworks.

Brackett's name is cut into it, along with a pattern much like Portland Wreath.

Olive green blown-glass lamp with matching shade.

Ruby-red blown lamp base made by William B. Wood for his sister.

Frank H. Swan Collection, Portland Museum of Art, Portland, Maine.

Many of the pressed patterns also were used on lamps. Several forms were made in Loop and Jewel, including an all-pressed, high-standard lamp, a hand lamp, and fonts mounted on milk glass bases with brass fittings between the two parts. Loop and Jewel fonts also were used with brass bases, as were Frosted Leaf and Magnet and Grape fonts. The latter two patterns were also available with milk glass bases. Fine Cut and Block was made in three styles: a hand lamp, a tall standard lamp, and a tall standard lamp with a handle. All three forms could be clear, colored, or flashed in color. There are tall lamps in the Greek Key, O'Hara, and Oak Band patterns. Strangely enough, there does not seem to be a lamp in the very popular Tree of Life pattern, except for an odd lamp made from a compote standard with a clear blown

Lamp depicting lady's hand with bracelet.

Lamp in O'Hara pattern.

ont attached with a glass wafer. One of the arest of Portland lamps is the Child Samuel, which usually has a clear blown font but also an be found with a ruby font in a pattern that s a variation of the common thumbprint. Rose Band was made in a hand lamp.

The production of blown lamp chimneys was normous. Some of them were quite fancy and vere cut, etched, enameled, hand-painted, or ven flashed in a color or in gold.

Another category of lamps of special interest to the collector is a parlor lamp style known nowadays as Gone With The Wind. Indications are that these lamps were not made until the 1870's, which explains their scarcity, for by then the factory was already in decline. The name comes from the fact that lamps of this type were used everywhere in the film of Margaret Mitchell's *Gone With The Wind*. Some of the loveliest Gone With The Wind lamps were produced by the Portland Glass Company, and fortunately they were signed

Three Fine Cut and Block lamp styles.
Swischer Collection

on the brass base with "P.G. Co." Even the brasswork was done right at the factory. Most, but not all, have a raised, puffy pattern in the glass and are beautifully hand-enameled in delicate colors.

Being a progressive company, Portland Glass also made shades for the new gaslights. Among the patterns in which these were made are Crackle, Ophidian, Hobnail with Yellow Rim, Tree of Life, and Paris.

Shield hand lamp.

Lamp with painted chimney, patented by Levi F. Drake and Enoch Egginton (#72376, issued December 17, 1867).

Frank H. Swan Collection, Portland Museum of Art, Portland, Maine.

Quartered Block lamp with painted chimney. The painted designs may differ somewhat. Look for the white band with blue at the top and for the floral decoration in these colors.

Open Salts

Open salts, like lamps, were special items. They often were made in the standard patterns, but they also were made as individual pieces. Some were blown, many were pressed, and a few were cut. Open-salt patterns include Loop and Jewel, Leverne, Tree of Life, Squirrel, Fine Cut and Block, Shell and Tassel, Ophidian, and Dahlia.

Some of the individual pieces have become justly famous among salt collectors. The Crossed Logs, for example, is well known and very typical of Portland Glass. Perhaps the most sought-after salt is Nest in Branches, which is exactly what it sounds like—a bird's nest held high in the branches of the stand, with the word Salt in raised letters on the nest. (This sometimes is known as Salt in Branches.) Many lesser known salts take their themes from nature. We were unable to locate an unusual one made in the form of a tree trunk with a snake coiled around it, but its companion toothpick holder appears in an accompanying photograph.

The little green jewel-like salt illustrated is a fine example of a blown and cut salt. The design is common, but the execution is quite exceptional.

Salts are a wonderful medium for collecting Portland Glass, since even the apartment-dweller with limited space can find a spot for these diminutive pieces. Even for those who decide to expand into salt shakers (which are available in several patterns), the space requirements remain small.

Dark amber salt (no pattern name).

Leverne salt.

Squirrel master salt.

Oak Band salt.

Two Crossed Log salts; O'Hara salt in center.

Green cut-glass salt.

Salt in Branches.

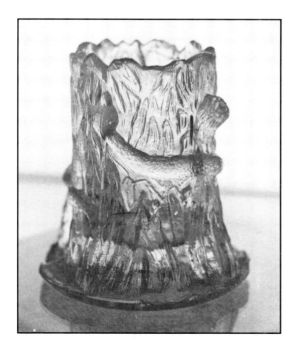

Odd toothpick holder. The matching salt looks like the lower third with the snake's head at rim.

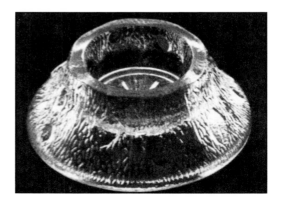

Tree Stump salt.

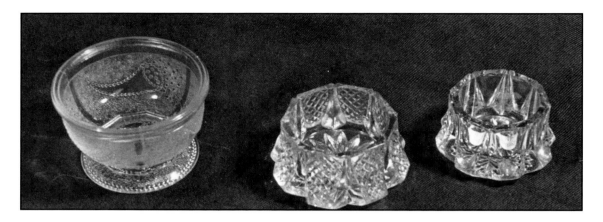

Salts: Powder and Shot; variant of Portland; Portland.

Two Ophidian salts in silver holders; Crackle miniature rose bowl.

An old photograph of a Tree of Life salt. Irregularly shaped cells are absent, but triangular shapes are the same, and center band is clear.

Good Luck salt.

Chapter 7

Cut Glass

Exquisitely fashioned lantern made for C.P. Brackett, watchman at the Portland Glass Company. Fittings are heavy brass.

Frank H. Swan Collection, Portland Museum of Art, Portland, Maine.

Although pressed glass was without a doubt the major product of the Portland Glass Company, intaglio cut glass[1] also was important. As mentioned earlier, a great deal of cut glass was made, but until recently it was impossible to identify. Now more is known about it, but the full extent of the factory's cut-glass output may never be known.

The main reason why cut-glass patterns are difficult to research is that cut patterns were not named. We have assigned names to the Portland cut patterns in order to help with the task of identification. Because of this longtime lack of names, the only sources of information are people who have items that are signed or can be traced to the factory (for example, pieces given to the Portland Museum of Art by Miss Margaret Tolman).

As with most manufacturing techniques, there are different methods of cutting glass. The method employed most frequently at Portland involved the use of copper disks charged with emery powder and oil and rotated at high speed. The resultant cutting was sharp yet shallow and capable of producing fine detail. This type of cutting, usually referred to as intaglio, is often mistakenly called etching. Since both intaglio and etching techniques were used at Portland Glass—sometimes even to create similar patterns—it is important to know the differences between them.

With etching, the surface of the glass is merely frosted, using acid. Although this area feels different from the surrounding glass, the surface is not indented. With cutting (or intaglio), a groove is cut into the glass, changing the surface plane of the cut area. It is easy to feel that the pattern is cut and that the glass is indented.

With some patterns, cutting is only a part of the overall technique, while a few patterns are produced entirely by cutting. Of the patterns that include some cutting, Sebago is deeply cut. (This pattern is covered in the chapter on frosted glass.) Honeycomb, Globe and Star, and Shell and Tassel sometimes have fern cutting or etching. When Honeycomb is cut, it usually is flint glass. Custom initial or monogram cutting is used on Tree of Life and Magnet and Grape. The horizontal lines on Rose Band are nearly always cut.

The styles discussed in detail in this chapter are those in which the entire pattern is produced by cutting. In most instances, these patterns are applied to blown flint glass. The forms a graceful and made of relatively thin glass of gre brilliance and clarity. The quality of the cutti itself ranges widely from good to superb.

The four patterns in this category a Cathedral Rose, White Iris, Portland Wreat and Cut Fern. The first one traced to t Portland factory was the one that we nam Portland Wreath, and the most recent discovered one is White Iris. Perhaps more c patterns will come to light, but in t meantime, these four patterns are among t finest glass produced at the Portland Gla Company, and they should have an honor spot in every Portland Glass collection.

Cathedral Rose spooner, signed "E. Egginton, Dec. 1863." This rare item is similar to a set of stemware made for Mrs. Abraham Lincoln.

Cathedral Rose

Cathedral Rose is Enoch Egginton's masterpiece, created for First Lady Mary Todd Lincoln. Unfortunately, there are few existing examples of this charming pattern. We are fortunate that our collection includes a beautiful spooner signed "E. Egginton, Dec. 1863," purchased from the Egginton family.

Just prior to Egginton's arrival in Portland, he was commissioned by Mrs. Lincoln to design and create a set of stemware. According to Egginton's diary, most of the set was completed before he arrived in Portland, but some items broken in shipment had to be replaced. A few additional items were also made for the set. It was a delicate, elegant pattern and would cost $4,000—a great deal of money at the time. Just how many pieces Mrs. Lincoln received for that amount is unknown, but it is certain that the pattern is just what she asked for. The inspiration for the pattern was a bush of a well-known rose of the era.

The glass itself is the finest-quality flint, with a ring that resembles a cathedral bell in a distant valley. The stemware was blown in three pieces, and the base, stem, and bowl are beautifully joined. The base is clear, with a polished pontil, while the stem is clear and spool-shaped—a very simple design that emphasizes the exquisite bowl.

The bowl is a classic shape, narrowing slightly at the top. In all forms except the goblet, the rim is delicately scalloped. The glass of the bowl, while thin, is not too much so. About one-half inch down from the rim is a frosted band not quite one-quarter inch wide. Another fine band is below it, with a third slightly wider band below that, just touching the tops of the cathedral arches that circle the piece. The arches are pointed, with just the tops of the points cut off by the third band.

Each arch is one inch high and one inch wide, created by two frosted bands one-eighth inch wide and slightly overlapping along their length. Where the sides of the arch come together at the top is a clear diamond. Two clear diamonds are at the bottom, where adjacent arches cross, forming a pick. From each pick, a garland falls one and a half inches before curving back up to touch the opposite pick of the arch. The arch and garland together produce an elongated oval one inch by two and a half inches. At the center of each oval is a full blown rose sprig. Interspaced in the roseleaf garland are many tiny, very shallow cut tendrils, which are visible only on very close examination.

Even an inexperienced eye will notice that this pattern required great craftsmanship and care to produce. Cathedral Rose is a pattern not found very often, but it is a prize worth searching for.

White Iris

This is another cut-glass pattern recently identified as made by the Portland Glass Company. In discussing a name for it, we first thought of the obvious one, fleur-de-lis, but then we decided that since the fleur-de-lis is a stylized white iris, that name would be more appropriate to a pattern reminiscent of that lovely spring flower.

White Iris goblet, signed "J. Egginton, Feb. 1864."

The goblet shown in the accompanying photograph is a blown flint, one of superb quality. In addition to the delicate fleur-de-lis cutting, there is the same banding at the top as in the Cathedral Rose pattern. The stem, too, is quite similar to that of Cathedral Rose. We found this goblet in an antique shop tucked away on a back shelf. It was so dirty that it was hard to see the lovely cutting, but the shape was particularly attractive. At home, we examined it closely and realized that what was appealing was its similarity to Cathedral Rose. Washing produced another surprise: the piece was signed and dated 1864. Not only that, but it proved to be the first known piece signed by Joseph Egginton, foreman of the cutting room at the Portland Glass Company and brother of the creator of Cathedral Rose! We have found more White Iris pieces since then,

and Egginton descendants also have a set twelve goblets, but this is the only sign one—a real treasure.

Portland Wreath

Portland Wreath is the most common the cut patterns. Quite a few authenticat pieces exist in a range of shapes in bo pressed and blown glass. Goblets, whic occur in a variety of styles, are perhaps t most frequently found form. All have cle bases and stems. The stems may be straig flared to the bottom, or may even have knob. All of them are cut and flare to t top, forming petals on the bottom of t bowl, as in the Casco pattern. Most of t stems are hexagonal.

The cutting for this pattern is in the form two branches of leaves that cross at t bottom and form a wreath that is not clos

Portland Wreath cut goblet (alternate shape).

Portland Wreath cut goblet.

Portland Wreath cut goblet (alternate shape).

at the top. The leaf branches are interrupted in the middle by one or two small flowers, which may have five or six petals each. The center of the flower may have solid frosting or crosshatched lines.

Since this pattern often was used for gifts or presentation pieces, there usually is an Old English initial in the center of the wreath. All of the blown-glass examples are of fine quality flint. Most of the pressed examples are also flint, but of a lesser quality. Although they are rare, nonflint examples do exist.

In addition to goblets, you may find any form that also was made in Etched Fern. Blown items were made in many unusual forms, and often they were one-of-a-kind. Close examination of the wreath will produce the identification. If the wreath is the right one, the form is not important.

Cut Fern sugar and creamer.

Cut Fern

Cut Fern is a fairly common pattern. The version seen most often has a band of fern fronds much like Etched Fern. Usually the Cut Fern design was used rather than the etched one on flint glass or large forms in the nonflint glass. All of the forms used for Portland Wreath may be found with the Cut Fern pattern.

In addition to forms with the ordinary fern band, there are some with vertical fern fronds. These items are nearly always on flint glass, and often there are monograms on them. A rare creamer (see Appendix II for photo) may be found with the same applied handle used on Globe and Star. Orbed Feet may sometimes have fern cutting.

Cut Fern on Honeycomb creamer
Marion P. Dana collection,
Portland Museum of Art.

Cut Overlay

Through the years we have seen many cut overlay objects that the owners have ascribed to the Portland Glass Co., however, there has never been a provable connection to the factory. The quality and designs were similar, if not identical to glass commonly attributed to the Sandwich Glass Company.

The situation has changed, there are at least two cut overlay objects which are without question products of the Portland Glass Co., The aspect of these items would tend to indicate that all the items claimed as Portland products may well have been produced at the glass house on Casco Bay.

One item of which there can be no doubt is an extremely lovely cranberry cut to clear 11" chalice made of heavy flint glass of great brilliance. The piece was made as a presentation to Charles Jose, a Portland merchant and one of the founders of the Portland Glass Company. It has, until recently, been in his family.

The second item is an extremely beautiful lamp in milk white glass cut through to deep amethyst. Its handsome shade is frosted cut to clear with the cutting flashed deep purple.

Cut Overlay chalice made for Charles Jose.

Overlay lamp, white cut to amethyst marble and bronze base.

Chapter 8

The Tree of Life Group:
Portland's Best–Known Patterns

Tree of Life Hand compote in an exceptionally deep sapphire blue.

Without question, the family of patterns known as the Tree of Life group represents the Portland Glass Company's major claim to fame. Tree of Life itself was one of the most popular designs of all time. It was copied widely and remains a favorite of collectors today. Although none of the other members of the family ever gained the popularity of Tree of Life, they were some of the most interesting and distinctive patterns produced.

Members of the Tree of Life group are Tree of Life with Sprig, Tree of Life, Ophidian, Crackle, Lotus/Garden of Eden, Tree of Life Milk Glass, and Horsehead Medallion.

Tree of Life with Sprig

This pattern probably is the forerunner of the more famous Tree of Life. When new ideas were being developed at the Portland factory, it was common practice to develop several similar patterns and try them out. It also was common for the company to create new patterns by modifying existing ones.

We are certain the Tree of Life, as it is recognized today, was developed during the early part of the superintendency of William O. Davis. It now seems evident that Davis did not invent the design but rather developed it from a pattern made at Portland before he arrived there. The earlier pattern was Tree of Life with Sprig; it can definitely be ascribed to the factory's beginning. A reporter for the *Eastern Argus,* April 16, 1864, described the pattern in detail, even though no name was attached to it.

Among this pattern's major design elements, as seen in the accompanying photograph of a water pitcher, is a lower segment with the Tree of Life pattern. Close examination reveals that the tiny triangles are random rather than in groups of six—as seen later in the production form of Tree of Life. This lower

Tree of Life with Sprig water pitcher. It does not have the small wheels found on the creamer and milk pitcher.

Tree of Life with Sprig sugar bowl. The finial is unlike that on any other Portland pattern.

segment is surmounted by a clear ring. The body has fluted segments with a wide side panel decorated with a slender spray of two kinds of leaves, somewhat like those found on Tree of Life Milk Glass items. In the center are two bell-shaped flowers that resemble small lilies of the valley. The handle is a typical Portland style, being a simulation of a tree branch. It should be noted that the creamer and milk pitcher have two curious little flat disks just below the handle. The upper one is larger, and both are spoked like a wheel. These apparently serve no purpose.

As is often the case with prototype patterns, the number of forms is limited. The only items we have seen in this pattern are the water pitcher, milk pitcher, and the table set consisting of sugar, spooner, creamer, and butter dish.

Tree of Life

When writing about the Tree of Life pattern, it is difficult not to overdo the superlatives. This was the most widely known pattern made at the Portland factory and the only pressed one that was ever signed. It appealed to the Victorian taste because of the extensive range of colors and forms available.

The name of this pattern has its roots in antiquity. The tree, of course, is one of the great influences in the life of man. It provides many of the basic needs of society, including shelter, warmth, and food. The motif probably originated in Persia, and it certainly has biblical connections. In Genesis 2:9 we read, "And out of the ground the Lord God made to grow every tree that is pleasant to the sight and good for food, the tree of life also in the midst of the garden, and the tree of the knowledge of good and evil." Revelation 22:2 refers to "the tree of life with its twelve kinds of fruit, yielding its fruit each month; and the leaves of the tree were for the healing of the nations." How appropriate that the Portland Glass Tree of Life concentrated its attention on the leaves of this wonderful tree; the United States certainly needed healing powers during that polarizing period of the Civil War!

A good indication of the importance of this pattern was the fact that it was one of only three that the Portland Glass Company patented. Throughout the entire glass industry, it was not common practice to patent patterns. Despite the patent, however, patterns such as Tree of Life were copied quickly by other companies. The Sandwich and Pittsburgh glass firms, for example, made minor changes in the design to evade the patent rights, and soon they were producing their own versions of Tree of Life. The Sandwich version, in fact, was an exact copy of one of Portland's prototype patterns that

The first pieces in the authors' collection: Tree of Life.

Pequot footed sauce; Tree of Life Hand compote.

was made in the form of a compote and occasionally is found with the Davis signature. The prototype pattern also was used at Portland for such other items as the round salt illustrated in the section on open salts and the knobs of Horsehead Medallion.

The true Portland Tree of Life pattern also was produced at Sandwich, as evidenced by excavation at the Sandwich factory site. This situation probably occurred in two ways. First, the Portland and Sandwich factories were on friendly terms and cooperated when one had more orders than it could handle. Because of this, excavation of the Portland factory site probably would unearth fragments of patterns known to be Sandwich patterns. Second, the Tree of Life molds were sold to Sandwich when the Portland factory closed, so the very popular pattern continued to be made at that factory.

Tree of Life was made in an extensive variety of forms. The total number of known shapes and sizes now stands at sixty-seven, the most for any single pattern. This number probably will increase, since previously unknown items are being found constantly. Almost as varied as the forms were the colors, ranging in the

yellowish green, from pale straw to deep canary yellow and including yellow-green, vaseline, pale apple green, and deep bottle green. In the blue range are pale aqua, light blue, brilliant deep sapphire, and even deeper cobalt. Deep purple, ruby, cranberry, and raspberry shades, while rare, do exist, as does a color that approaches orange. All shades of amber abound. Every color produced at Portland was used for Tree of Life, and some colors are exclusively found in this pattern. The accompanying illustrations show as wide a variety as possible of the colors available.

Although there seems to be no doubt that the Tree of Life pattern originated at the Portland Glass Company, there is considerable doubt about the designer of the pattern. It has always been assumed that the designer was William O. Davis, since his signature is the one that usually appears on it. But there is increasing evidence that, as mentioned above in the discussion of the Tree of Life with Sprig pattern, Davis did not create this pattern but merely borrowed a design element from the prototype design introduced by Enoch Egginton. What Davis contributed to the Tree of Life pattern was the extraction of disarmingly simple repeat design from the more complex parent. He then expanded that to cover the surface of the glass.

The immediate success of Tree of Life led to the introduction of such patterns as Ophidian (a combination of the Tree of Life and Crackle patterns) and Shell and Tassel, another very popular design.

The Portland Glass Company, innovative in many ways, was one of the first to sign its products. Other companies later marked or signed pattern glass, but as mentioned above, Tree of Life was the first pattern to be signed. Some forms are marked "P.G. Co. Patent." The marking appears on the smooth side of the glass, which can be either the top or the the bottom, depending on the individual form. Most signed forms also exist in unsigned versions. Among the marked items are compotes, goblets, wines, lemonades, sauce dishes, honeys, sugars, creamers, spooners, butter dishes, cake stands, ice cream trays, and vases.

Amber and apple-green ribbed finger bowls.

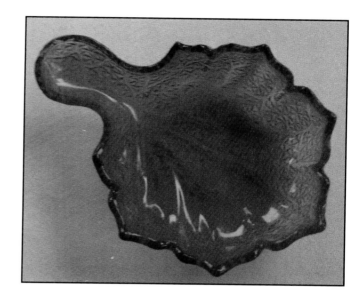

Tree of Life red sauce (rare in this color.)

Canary Tree of Life ice cream set.

Tree of Life goblet and lemonade, signed P.G. Co.

Another method of marking Tree of Life was to incorporate the name "Davis" into the branch ornamentation, thus causing a slight rearrangement of the pattern. Items signed in this way are often difficult to detect, because the name seems to fade into the design. Most likely to be signed in this manner are the

**Tree of Life handled wine
in very rare purple.**
Collection of Portland
Museum of Art, Portland, Maine.

the Portland patent marking, so in a way the Portland Glass Company lives on.

Even a signature on a piece of glass is no guarantee that it was actually made in the Portland factory, since it could have been made at Sandwich or elsewhere after Portland closed. After handling a great deal of Portland Glass, it becomes possible to identify it simply by its feel and look. This is not something that can be taught in the pages of a book; it can be learned only by continued exposure to specimens of the glass. But it is quite apparent that the quantity of Tree of Life produced at Sandwich was quite small and specimens of it are fairly easily detectable by glass experts.

And now to attempt a description of this indefinable pattern. The design basically is made up of a series of branches that intersect, forming a series of irregularly shaped cells. These cells are filled with little triangular forms arranged in groups of six, thus creating hexagonal minicells within the main cell. Although the smallest elements of the design have been referred to as triangles, they are actually tiny pyramids with one face to the back. Thus, what appear to be triangles are in fact three-dimensional, with one corner of the

larger and more important forms, such as compotes, cake stands, trays and epergnes. The hand compote has never been found signed while the Child Samuel epergne and cake stand are always signed.

The idea of an epergne (a flower or fruit holder) was one of the Portland innovations that had great impact on the American glass industry. Many Portland epergnes were marked "P.G. Co. Patent." This did not refer to the Tree of Life patent but a patent on the idea of an epergne. A license for manufacture was granted when the patent application was pending, so the glass was marked as though the patent had been granted. Portland's patent was sold to another glass company whose identity is unknown, and it in turn licensed other companies to make epergnes under the patent. Thus, we often find epergnes that obviously were made by other companies but are marked "P.G. Co. Patent, April 20, 1875," in just recognition of Portland's patent. Even today, there are new glass epergnes with

**Detail of Tree of Life leaf
sauce in red.**

**Davis signature on Tree of Life
(photograph enhances signature).**

...yramid pointing straight out. The Portland Tree of Life is a well-defined and sharply pressed pattern that has been described by several writers as fernlike, although we fail to see this resemblance.

Even though the pattern was imitated at other factories with minor changes, the Portland product is far superior, not only in the glass quality but also in the classic beauty of the forms produced. It has been our observation that the other factories produced a very limited number of forms in the pattern, and then only in clear glass. For some time, it was thought that ribbed or melon–shaped bowls were never made at Portland, even though the samples exhibited all the traits of the factory. Now it appears that these bowls were indeed made at Portland, and in fact made nowhere else!

The stemware in this pattern is particularly handsome, ranging from tiny finger cordials to beautifully styled goblets. Some of the features that quickly distinguish the Portland goblets are the ball in the stem bisected by a clear glass band (this is also visible in the knobs of the covered pieces), the unusually tall bowl design, and the clear and unadorned half-inch bands at the rim. Goblets and other items with Old English letters in a shield were made as special items for Christmas or other gift-giving occasions. The goblets were made in several sizes, all in the same style, and were often marked "P.G. Co. Patent," as were the footed tumblers or lemonades.

Among the most impressive items in the

Tree of Life pattern are compotes and epergnes. For many years, it was thought, that although the pattern of the hand compotes was obviously Portland in character, they were made at Pittsburgh. We now know that this is not true.[1] These interesting items depict a lady's hand holding up the bowl of the compote, which comes in three sizes. Usually they are clear, but occasionally they can be found in an exciting shade of sapphire. The hand may be clear glass with a frosted base, or the reverse, or even all clear. Two sizes of cake stands as well as a small epergne with a clear glass fluted vase also were made in this design. Items with a baby's hand, or with a hand used as the handle of a pitcher, are not Portland Glass, nor is a lady's hand without the bracelet. These items are, usually, of such poor-quality glass that it would be difficult to mistake them for Portland.

Compotes in three sizes, epergnes, and large cake stands can also be found in Tree of Life with the standard depicting a child holding a

Child Samuel Tree of Life compote.

book. This is the well–known Child Samuel of the Bible, and it is shown here in canary yellow. Child Samuel usually is found in clear glass, occasionally in canary yellow or vaseline, and very rarely in apple green. Other colors may well exist, but they have not come to our attention.

The Child Samuel variation, like Tree of Life itself, is a Biblical origin. Samuel, of course, was the last of the judges, the first of the prophets, and, next to Moses, the greatest personality in the early history of the Israelites. Samuel's mother begged the Lord to be blessed with a man child, in return for which she would give the child to the Lord. The Child Samuel motif depicts him as he was presented by his mother to the Lord, with long hair and dressed in a robe that his mother bought him. Any collector of American glass would cherish such a piece.

Not all compotes, epergnes, and cake stands are this fancy. Most have a simple Tree of Life standard with a bowl that may be clear glass or Tree of Life. Examples found might be molded in a single piece or two pieces joined directly or with a wafer.

Design elements from successful patterns often were incorporated into other patterns. Even Tree of Life was not immune from this practice, and it received a gift from Loop and Jewel in the form of the round ornamentation used on the edge of the plates. (Plates were also made without this embellishment.)

Some of the more curious items made only in Tree of Life are lovely colored tiles designed to be used as ornamental inserts in such things as furniture and iron stoves. The tiles were three–or four–inch squares or circles and are considered prizes when found today. One crisp fall day, we went to Proctor, Vermont, to look for some of these tiles that we had been told were used in a unique manner—as the central panels of a stained–glass window. We arrived at the nineteenth-century Wilson

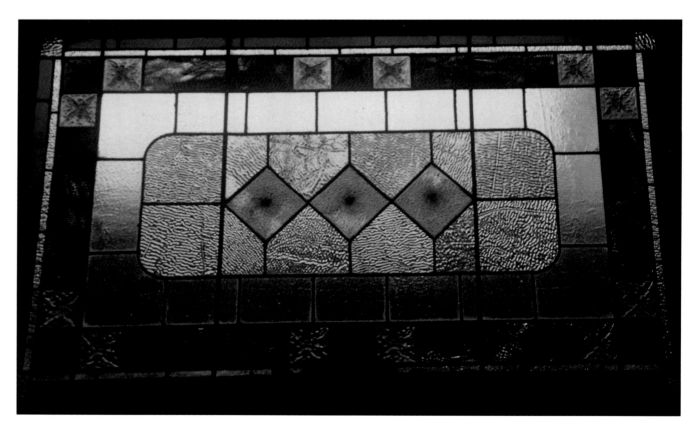

Stained Glass window in Wilson castle, Proctor, Vermont. Tree of Life in center.

Castle, an imposing and rather unlikely place open to the public. After taking a guided tour of the castle, we were disappointed not to have seen the objects of our visit. We then asked Mr. Wilson, the owner, if he knew the location of the window we were seeking; we had been told it was in a bedroom. He assured us that it was not in his castle. We asked if we could look at some of the bedrooms that had not been included in the tour, and he very graciously accompanied us in our search. Just as we were about to give up, we came upon it. It was a breathtaking sight in the late–afternoon sun. Three panels of beautiful aquamarine were set in the center of a window surrounded by very lovely purple and lavender glass. We now have reason to believe not only that these central panels were produced at the Portland Glass Company, but that the entire window was made there—as were many of the lovely stained–glass windows in grand homes in Portland. In fact, the Portland factory had a full-time window maker named Dennis Cole.[2] Just another facet of an altogether fascinating company!

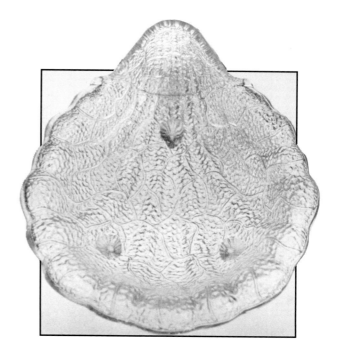

Tree of Life shell bowl with rolled edge. Three applied feet are visible through the glass.

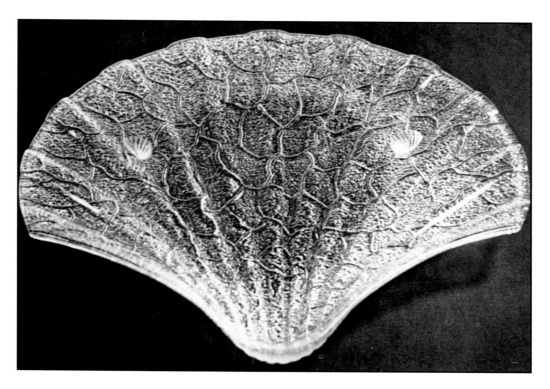

Tree of Life shell flat platter with applied feet.

Peacock blue sugar in silver holder with peacock finial.

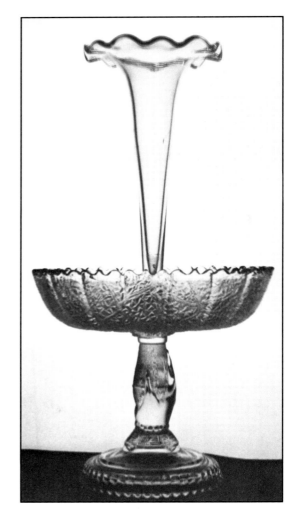

Small Tree of Life epergne with hand base.

Tree of Life creamer in silver holder by J. Babcock.

**Large single epergne in Tree
of Life pattern.**

Tree of Life basket in silver, signed Davis.

Tree of Life sugar.

Tree of Life leaf shaped sauces.

61

Tree of Life patterns: Portland (left), Pittsburgh (center), and Sandwich (right). There is strong evidence that all three forms originated at Portland. It is certain that all three were made at Portland and probably were three prototypes. When the form on the left was patented, the other two (which were unprotected) were copied.

Forms In Which Tree Of Life Was Made

uttermilk goblet* · water goblet* · wine goblet*
laret · champagne · finger cordial
monade* · footed tumbler* · cider mug
ddy mug · single egg cup · double egg cup
oted master salt* · footed individual salt · flat salt
utter chip · 3" plate · 5" plate
' plate* · 8" plate · 8" candlestick
hamber stick* · large leaf sauce · small leaf sauce
auce dish* · round berry bowl · straight finger bowl
' ribbed shallow bowl · 5" ribbed shallow bowl · 6" ribbed shallow bowl
' ribbed shallow bowl · 8" ribbed shallow bowl · 9" ribbed shallow bowl
0" ribbed shallow bowl · 11" ribbed shallow bowl · 12" ribbed shallow bowl
nger bowl, melon shape · ice cream tray* · 8" compote*
' compote* · 10" compote* · Child Samuel compote*
' hand compote · 8" hand compote · 9" hand compote
nall single epergne* · medium single epergne · large single epergne*
vo-tiered epergne* · three-tiered epergne · water pitcher
vered sugar* · creamer* · spooner*
vered butter dish* · footed oval bowl · honey dish
rge shell dish, rolled edge · mustard pot · shell bowl, rolled edge
val relish · 8" cake stand · 9" cake stand
2" cake stand · round tile · square tile
asket, applied handle · covered bowl · covered compote*
ine cooler · small vase · medium vase
rge vase* · celery · powder jar
air receiver · oil lamp · Child Samuel epergne*

Tree Of Life Forms Found In Silver Holders

ugar* · creamer · sweetmeat
elery · compote · water pitcher
ickle caster · double relish
ride's basket* · spooner

indicates items that may be signed.

Ophidian

Ophidian is probably the most unusual and fascinating pattern produced at the Portland factory. Earlier writers called this pattern Tree of Life Variant for lack of a specific name, but we feel that it is totally different and deserves its own pattern name. We have taken the liberty of calling the pattern Ophidian in recognition of what often is the most startling feature of an otherwise-simple design: the brilliantly colored and beautifully gilded blown serpents twined around the icelike glass. We hope that by giving this design a name, we can clear up the confusion that exists among collectors, since few of them know what Tree of Life Variant refers to. Most people assume it is a reference to the other Tree of Life patterns made in Pittsburgh and Sandwich.

It has long been assumed that the red cobalt, white, and green serpents wer occasionally added to the more importan forms as a whimsey and that they were not standard feature of the pattern. It no appears that this is not true; the serpent indeed were a standard and important part the pattern. It is evident to us that th unadorned items were intended to be use with the serpent forms, and when the two a mixed, it becomes a set of extraordinar beauty and interest. It has been reported tha a complete set with red serpents was ordere by the governor of Massachusetts, but this only partly true. The set used in th Massachusetts State House consisted of a four available colors plus unadorned item with the central piece being a magnificent pa

Two-tiered epergne in Ophidian.
Frank H. Swan Collection,
Portland Museum of Art, Portland, Maine.

of two-tiered epergnes, one in red (like the one now at the Portland Museum of Art) and one in green. These epergnes are truly impressive, eleven inches in diameter and twenty inches tall, with a snake coiled around the upper section and another coiled around the lower section. Smaller pieces were unable to support such elaborate decoration, and so were unadorned.

It is worthwhile at this point to note the distinction between Ophidian and Tree of Life. Ophidian is almost completely random, without precision and order of formed cells and little triangles that characterize Tree of Life. Careful examination of Ophidian, however, reveals why it is considered a variation of Tree of Life. The amorphous shapes are divided into random cells formed by the branchlike veinings. When the two patterns are viewed side by side, it is obvious that they are from the same family. The serpent adornment of Ophidian, then is quite appropriate.

The most often asked question about Portland Glass is, "Why the obsession with

Scalloped berry bowl and leaf dish in Ophidian.

serpents?" Many of the motifs of Portland Glass are derived from nature, and the serpent is, after all, a creature that sparks both fascination and aversion in mankind. In Portland Glass, the major use of the serpent is in the Ophidian pattern, but it is also found on Opaline and occasionally on Crackle, on a small rare Banded Portland vase, as well as on two very seldom found salts and toothpick

Ophidian: two styles of goblets and a compote.

Ophidian 14" vase.

Rare Ophidian nautilus shell in branches, signed "E. C. Beals, Christmas 1869."

holders (see section on Open Salts). The Garden of Eden pattern also has a representation of a serpent head.

Ophiolatry has its roots deep in man's past. Many primitive people have worshiped the serpent in many forms, possibly reaching a zenith in the Maya and Inca cultures. Serpent worship was common in the majority of the Indian cultures as well as in many African and Asian societies. Those of us with a Judaeo-Christian background will, of course, recognize in Portland Glass serpents the biblical symbolism of the serpent in the Garden of Eden.

When used on smaller glass pieces, serpents become much less impressive. Some owners of the Ophidian cheese dish, in fact, have not been amused to have their serpent described as a beautifully marked worm. Indeed, the gold markings are beautifully executed, making the Portland serpents easy to identify and distinguish from items of other manufacture and decidedly inferior quality. Although it cannot be proven absolutely, we believe that the true Ophidian pattern was made only at Portland, despite many claims to the contrary. It is certain that no other source has ever been established.

This pattern exhibits many fine qualities. It is always made of the finest-quality glass in crystal clear, straw, raspberry, chartreuse, cranberry, and occasionally in a glorious shade of aqua. After examination of a great many pieces in this pattern, we have come to the conclusion that the edges always were flashed with gold. We have seen many articles with gold lacking but have always found

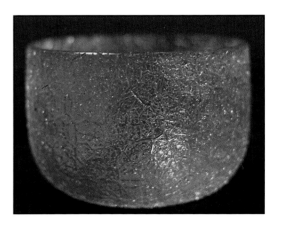

Chartreuse Ophidian finger bowl.

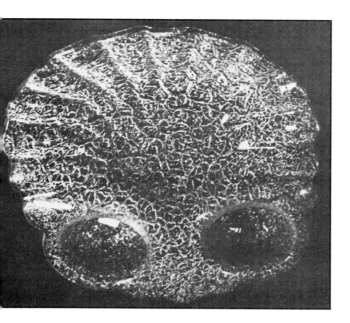

Ophidian condiment server.

ndications that it once had existed.

Very often, Ophidian items have silver holders. The list of forms and sizes is extensive, with many unusual items found in no other pattern. Among these are a double-handled butter tub and matching double-handled cheese dish, a wine cooler, a small cask, a dresser set, and gas lamp shades. A giant punch bowl with underplate is truly impressive, with crown-shaped scalloping and wide gold edging. The punch cups are cask-shaped, with applied handles that may be clear glass or colored serpents. Another exceptional item is a water pitcher with a freeform rim. A serpent is wrapped around the entire pitcher and then lifts from the surface to form the handle before biting into the rim. Also exceptional is a beautifully shaped cracker jar with a coiled serpent on the lid.

Still another unique aspect of the production of this pattern is the fact that it took the full range of the glassblower's art to execute it. Many items are pressed, some are blown molded, some use both techniques and are put together with wafers. Some are free blown, many have applied handles and decorations. The candlesticks (13" and 18") exhibit all of the techniques.

Other items that include a serpent are a cake stand in three sizes, stemware in many sizes from cordials to wines, to champagnes, water and buttermilk goblets, footed sugar and creamer, spooner (spoonholder), covered compote, footed salt, and finger bowl. Items found without the serpent embellishment are plates in three sizes (6", 8½", and 9½"). With gold rims and sometimes with round ornaments, sauce dishes, salt and pepper in a holder, honey dish, butter chip, platters in three sizes, water tray, mugs, finger bowls, and the complete range of stemware.

The first enameled glass acquired by the authors. Wine set with Ophidian base. Green blown decanter and cordials with enamel decoration.

Crackle

This pattern, generally considered part of the Tree of Life family, is based on a traditional pattern that we feel probably originated with the Venetians, was copied by the Bohemians, and finally spread throughout Europe. A similar pattern produced by the Sandwich Glass Company was called Overshot, which is the name often used for both it and the Portland pattern, even though the Portland product is slightly different. Close examination of the Portland pattern reveals the fine veinings that make it part of the Tree of Life group.

Handled wines Tree of Life and Ophidian.

Crackle raspberry tankard with applied handle.

Crackle cranberry dish in pewter holder.

Sugar bowl in shape of fruit.

The usual production method for Crackle was to roll the inflated gather over a marver board that had been covered generously with crushed glass fragments, thus producing the iced effect. Many people have questioned whether this product, in fact, was made at the Portland factory, but if we can believe the newpapers of the era, that should dispel any doubts. One *Eastern Argus* reporter who had just toured the factory mentions (May 28, 1866) that a particularly attractive vase was made by "coating the hot glass with small crushed or broken glass." This could only refer to the production of the Crackle pattern.

Also, several forms in a lovely shade o raspberry have been traced to the factory. Thi pattern can also be found in clear, straw cranberry, and pale aqua.

Crackle has been found in many forms including sauce dishes (both round and lea shapes), berry bowl, goblets (three sizes) wines (two sizes), cordials, plates (6", 8", anc 9"), oval and round trays, finger bowls, sal shaker, sugar shaker, open salt, butter chips mugs (three sizes), wine cooler, decanter, cak stand, compote (open and covered), butte dish (covered), butter tub (sometimes called a ice bucket), sugar, creamer, spooner, celery

Crackle bud vase in silver holder.

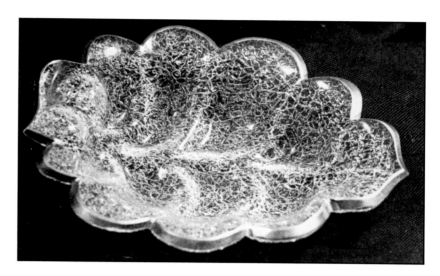

Crackle leaf relish dish with gold edge.

Crackle footed wines with gold rims.

Small Crackle compote with gold edge.

nd at least four vases. Perhaps the most nteresting are the table sets in the form of uits, in addition to their unique shapes they ften are found in special colors such as red r brilliant green.

To properly identify the Portland pattern, as opposed to Overshot patterns, look for the distinctive veining. The overshot effect may be produced in different ways, resulting in a totally different look, but all have the basic veining that sets them apart. The surface might be very sharp because of the applied crushed glass, or it might be smooth because the object was reheated to a point where the applied glass began to flow. There is also a variant (Ophidian) in which it appears that the entire pattern was produced in the pressing. The differences may be the result of a combination of factors. For instance, many of the patterns seem to have changed slightly after the 1867 fire that destroyed the first Portland factory. Also, there was, of course, a continuous process of refinement. The items that seem to have been totally pressed may have resulted from an effort to reduce the work involved and lower the cost. Judging from the way that set was expanded and embellished, this effect must have been popular. In fact, this effect eventually was used to create the Ophidian pattern just discussed. Ophidian was the link between Tree of Life and Crackle, as well as one of the most interesting products of old Casco. (Casco was an early name for Portland, a locale that also once bore such names as Machigonne, Indigreat, Elbow, The Neck, and Falmouth.)

Lotus/Garden of Eden

Usually, Lotus and Garden of Eden are treated as two patterns, but, in fact, they are variations of a single pattern. There has long been confusion over the name of this pattern, and it is often confused with Tree of Life, even though there is little similarity.

The design is perhaps best realized in the 10" oval bowl. The most obvious features of the pattern are the gracefully pointed lotus leaves that cover most of the bowl. Deep triangular grooves outline the leaves on the reverse side. The interior is filled with sharp stippling. The overall effect is a sharp, brilliant outline. Where the leaves come up to the clear rim, they create a kind of wave pattern that is also sharply outlined and very effective. At each end of the bowl is a lotus flower made up of petals executed in exactly the same way as the leaves. The petals surround an oval of clear glass crossed by three lines that intersect at the center of the oval. On each side is a seed pod covered with extremely fine stippling that is totally different from that used in the leaves and petals.

The Lotus goblets have a stem designed to

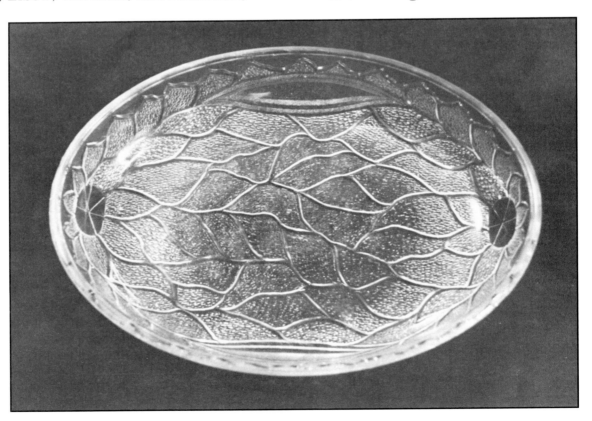

Lotus shallow oval bowl.

look like a tree trunk, as in the Owl and Possum pattern.

The only difference between the basic design and Garden of Eden is the addition of an animal head on some forms. There has been considerable discussion about the identification of this feature. Many people think it is a fish head, while others maintain it is the serpent in the Garden of Eden. We tend to think that it is just a turtle sticking its head out from amid the lotus. Whatever creature it is, its head is rather ugly.

We have always assumed that this pattern depicts the aquatic lotus of the Garden of Eden, but the goblet design might provoke the conclusion that it is in fact a Zizyphus lotus, the Mediterranean lotus tree whose fruits are said to be consumed by the "Lotus Eaters," the North African people who, according to Homer's Odyssey, live in an indolent, drugged state. Since this pattern is a product of the Portland Glass Company, however, it seems accurate to assume that the first interpretation is the correct one. An asterisk indicates items that may be found with a "turtle" head but also may be found unadorned.

Garden of Eden mug.

Lotus bread tray.

Garden of Eden goblet with serpent
head.

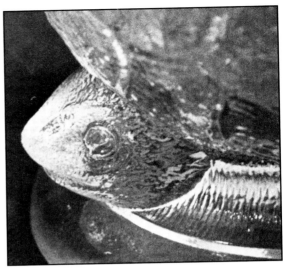

Close-up of serpent head on Garden of
Eden goblet.

Forms Found In The
Lotus/Garden Of Eden Pattern

oval relish
sauce dish
creamer*
butter dish*
compote
footed tumbler

10" oval bowl
water pitcher*
cake stand*
plate
decanter
pickle caster

berry bowl
milk pitcher*
sugar
honey
bread tray
lamp

* indicates items that may be found with a "turtle" head but also may be
found unadorned.

Tree of Life Milk Glass

This is a pattern made first at Portland Glass and then revived in the 1880's by Challinor Taylor Ltd., Tarentum, Pennsylvania. When made at Portland, the pattern was, we believe, made only in white and blue milk glass—with or without hand enameling. The later version was made in white, green, and blue milk glass. Close examination of the Challinor Taylor product reveals slight differences in the design of individual forms. It was not made in the Portland molds. Tree of Life Milk Glass is a beautiful pattern that commands high prices.

The number of forms made at Portland was limited. Most berry bowls and sauces were round, but some were bent while hot into a squared form, as shown in an accompanying photograph. What usually is called a rose jar actually is an oversize sugar. A larger piece in this same shape is a biscuit jar. A matching creamer and butter dish complete the set.

The design on the berry bowl is divided into six panels. Three panels on one side have a Tree of Life pattern with small flowers. When enameled, these flowers have one panel each of

Pickle caster, covered sugar, blue salt, cruet, white salt—all in Tree of Life Milk Glass.

yellow, pink, and blue. The leaves are in multiple shades of green with brown stems. The three panels on the opposite side have a daisy pattern with the same color schemes. The inside of the bowl often is enameled in cream.

All of the other forms have only three panels, with the Tree of Life in each panel. The same colors are used for the enameling.

Tree of Life Milk Glass: hand-enameled biscuit jar, berry bowl, and sauce dishes.

Free-form Tree of Life Milk Glass berry bowl made in same mold as more common berry bowl. Bowl was bent while still hot.

Horsehead Medallion

This pattern has not been authenticated as one of Portland Glass Company's, but it has long been attributed to Portland by writers on the subject of glass even without hard evidence. We have traced one item through a family claiming ties to the Portland factory. It is our policy, however, to require more than one such claim before accepting a pattern as proven. This pattern thus remains only a probable Portland design. It belongs to the Tree of Life family because it uses the Tree of Life design on finials and stem knobs. It is also an addition to the list of Portland patterns made in milk glass.

The major design element—from which the name is derived—is a stylized horse's head enclosed in a circular medallion of round ornaments. Between the medallions are sprigs of leaves much like the leaves on Tree of Life Milk Glass. The background is clear, as is the domed base. The glass is not flint, but it is fine and crystal clear. The milk glass forms are rare and priced high, as are the occasional pale green items.

LEFT: Horsehead Medallion celery vase.

Forms Found In Horsehead Medallion

covered butter
creamer
egg cup
toothpick
water pitcher
berry bowl

celery
covered compote
spooner
child's table set
tumbler
covered sugar

open sugar
open compote
goblet
sauce

Author's Maine Coon Cats. Sudko and Pandora, have catnip from an Ophidian bowl. The Coon cat is the official mascot of Maine.

Chapter 9

Patterns From Nature

Ophidian compote with green snake.

Motifs borrowed from nature are characteristic of the products of the Portland Glass factory. Many patterns have branchlike handles or feet, acorn finials, sunflower finials, or even snakes—even though the rest of the pattern is unrelated. This chapter covers the patterns that derive their major design element from nature.

Patterns with animals are Owl and Possum, Squirrel, and Deer and Pine. Patterns with woody plants are Dirigo Pear, Birch Leaf, Oak Leaf Band, Oak Leaf Medallion, and Acorn Band. The floral patterns are Rose Band and Dahlia.

Owl and Possum

This is perhaps the most unusual pattern created at the Portland factory, and it is one of the few patterns that has never been attributed to any other glass company. The goblet is the only form that is found readily today.

The pattern's basic shape is simple. The base is plain, and from it rises the stem in the form of a tree trunk, which is slightly bent.

(There need never be any confusion between the original and the reproduction because the makers of the reproduction thoughtfully straightened the stem.) The branches of the tree spread out from the top of the trunk to cover the bowl of the goblet.

The most startling features of this pattern are the two tiny embellishments on one side of the goblet. An owl sits on one of the branches, and opposite is a possum—hence, the name by which the pattern is known today. The factory, however, apparently did not consider these two little fellows particularly significant, because they named the pattern Winter Tree. A companion pattern, Summer Tree, had leaves on the branches shaped like those on Tree of Life Milk Glass, and in place of the owl and the possum were a bird and a squirrel. Although this pattern was mentioned in early accounts, no specimen of it has yet surfaced.

Our research has never produced any indication of the inspiration for this whimsical pattern. Perhaps it happened this way.

Owl side of Owl and Possum goblet.

Possum side of Owl and Possum goblet.

Fable of the Owl & Possum

The Owl and the Possum sat in a tree
On the shore of a lake, an inland Sea.
No thought they gave of Winter's cold embrace,
Two classy creatures content in this sunny place.

The golden days of Indian Summer soon passed.
Swiftly Winter came with a frosty blast.
Pale ice and cold moon froze them in crystal fast,
And that's how the Owl and Possum became
Portland Glass.

–T. L.–

Owl and Possum was made in a very limited number of forms. The water pitcher, the berry bowl (with feet exactly like those on the bowl in the Classic pattern), and footed sauces are the only other known forms. In fact, these last three forms are so rare that we have never seen a sauce dish and have only seen one example each of the pitcher and the berry bowl.

Squirrel/Squirrel in Bower

Of all the Portland patterns, this charming pattern causes perhaps the most confusion. This confusion arises from a series of water pitchers produced by the Indiana Tumbler and Goblet Company of Greentown, Indiana. No one seems to know just how many different patterns were produced in this Indiana series, but it should be clear to anyone who examines several of them—including the two most popular, "Squirrel" and Squirrel With Nut—that the Portland version is completely different in design and not a part of the series.[1]

It is unfortunate that the Portland factory called its pattern merely Squirrel, which is the same name applied to one of the Indiana patterns. This leads to considerable confusion. Adding to the confusion is the fact that because of the same names or because of the failure to recognize the Portland origin, some writers have given the name Squirrel in Bower to the Portland design. We see no

Squirrel pitcher.

Footed Squirrel berry bowl.

ason, however, why the original Portland
me should be abandoned, so we will refer to
e Portland product as Squirrel and to the
diana product as "Squirrel."

"Squirrel" is a pattern that depicts a squirrel
tting in a tree while another squirrel looks
r nuts on the ground. The base is clear, as is
e applied handle. Squirrel With Nut has a
mewhat larger squirrel sitting in a skimpy
ee eating a nut. These patterns were made
ly in pitcher and tumbler forms. The pitcher
s a clear handle and base, as have all the
hers that we have seen in this series. It has
en reported that other pieces were planned
the Indiana firm but never made because
a fire that destroyed all the molds in 1903.
The Portland Glass Squirrel is infinitely
ore interesting than the Indiana series. The
rry creature is seated in a rustic bower
rmed of tree branches arranged so as to
eate a pitched roof over his head. There are
rious other branches, plus the familiar

Portland oak leaves. The handle of the pitcher
is also typical Portland, being a representation
of a branch. At the rim is a rustic band that
also is branchlike, and the rustic motif is
continued at the base. Covered forms have a
squirrel as a finial.

Perhaps the best-known forms of Squirrel
are the open, individual and master salts.
They consist of a round salt in the form of a
cut-off tree trunk with a squirrel eating an
acorn used as a handle. On one of our trips
around Maine we stopped at an antiques
shop in Limerick. There, in the center of a
large table, was the finest Squirrel compote
we have ever seen: twelve inches in diameter
and fourteen inches high, with a three inch
squirrel sitting on top of the cover. He was so
realistic that we almost expected him to
scamper off across the oak branch. We have
never seen another Squirrel covered compote
and are still wondering why we failed to
purchase that one.

Forms In Which Squirrel Was Made

individual salt	master salt	water pitcher
goblet	tumbler	covered sugar
covered butter	creamer	spooner
footed sauce	berry bowl	compote

Deer and Pine

This recently confirmed pattern, also known as Deer and Doe, almost had to be Portland Glass just because of its name! Many collectors have suspected for some time that it was Portland, but now it has been traced to the factory.

The most unusual aspect of this pattern is its shape, which may be either rectangular or square. The goblet is the form most often encountered, and it is our model for the description of the pattern. The top of the bowl is round and clear. The bottom of the bowl, viewed from above, looks square. About an inch down from the rim, the bowl becomes flattened out into four panels. The front and back panels are perfectly flat, with the major design element—the two deer and the pine tree—shown in relief, with three rows of dots above the design. All of the panels are arched at the top and are separated by corner columns that also are capped with tiny arches. The end panels are slightly curved and clear, except for a row of diamond braid on each side and three vertical lines in the center that obscure the mold marks. The stem

is conical, growing smaller as it approach the clear base.

Whoever designed this pattern never looke very closely at a pine tree. The strange tree this design resembles a palm tree or a gia fern rather than a pine.

Among the forms in which Deer and Pi might be found are three open compotes, lar covered compote, water pitcher, goblet, win tumbler, bread tray, covered butter, suga creamer, spooner, trays (8"x13" and 11"x15 bowl, sauces, plates, cake stand, celery, ja jar, three mugs, and pickle dish. Only thr colors have been found: light blue, amber ar apple green. Displayed proudly in a Portla home is a complete set in apple green th was purchased at the factory.[2]

Rose Band

The name Rose Band was given to th interesting pattern by collector Frank Swa because the earlier name, Flower Band, wa shared with another pattern. We continue t use of Rose Band because of the confusio that would be caused by having a more wide known pattern of the same name.

Deer and Pine goblet.

Deer and Pine water pitcher.

Rose Band water pitcher and two tumblers.

Rose Band covered butter dish.

Rose Band holds a unique position in the list of Portland patterns. It is one of only two floral patterns produced, and is the only pattern that was cut after being pressed, giving it an elegant look. This is not an easy pattern to find, but it is worth pursuing, as it makes a lovely set. Each piece is a surprise and a delight.

Rose Band probably is one of the earliest patterns produced at the Portland factory, and, as far as we know, it was made only there and never reproduced. There are some indications that it was produced prior to the 1867 fire and not made after the fire.[3] The glass is of exceptional quality even though it tends to be thicker than most others. The pattern is deceptively simple until examined closely. There is a band of tiny, five petaled flowers and leaves slightly below the rim. The band, which varies in width depending on the size of the piece, had a background that is entirely different from any other Portland pattern. It is not frosted or stippled but made up of a series of rings, which are interrupted only by the floral decoration. In the finger cordials these rings are pressed, as is the rest of the pattern. In all of the larger forms, these rings or lines are beautifully cut. (Pieces are sometimes found without the cutting.) Below the band is a little scalloped edging, and below the scallop are vertical rows of notches that emanate from the points of the scallop and extend to the bottom of the piece. The bottom is rayed in typical Portland fashion.

The early demise of this charming pattern was no doubt due to the fact that the cutting was so time-consuming that it was too expensive to make.

Rose Band items you might expect to find are sauce dishes, berry bowl, water pitcher, tumblers, wines, cordials, sugar and creamer, butter dish, lamp, candy dish (with ring handle), plates, oval relish, celery, vases (three sizes), and cake stand. All forms made at Portland.

Rose Band open sugar and small vase.

Dahlia

This is the second of the two floral patterns made at the Portland Glass Company. It was produced in clear, apple green, light blue, dark blue, light amber, and dark amber. It has not been attributed to any other company, but it probably was made elsewhere, judging from the quantity of some forms of the clear product. Previous indications were that this pattern was made late in the factory's

Dahlia small mug.

Dahlia blue sauce dish. Background is tiny squares rather than stippling.

Dahlia covered sugar with gherkin finial.

Rare Dahlia pot de creme with gherkin finial.

existence. We now know that it was already in production in October of 1865.[4] We feel certain that the colored forms were made only at Portland.

Dahlia seems to be a pattern that is either loved or hated. There are many who collect it, yet other Portland Glass collectors have no interest in owning a piece of this pattern. It is unfortunate that it so closely resembles the Primrose pattern made by the Canton Glass Company in the 1880's: the two are often confused.

This is a very simple pattern, consisting of single blossoms separated by a band of leaves in clear glass against what seems at first to be a stippled background. Close examination, however, reveals that the background is a fine mesh design rather than the more common stippling. The overall appearance is of a brilliant, sparkling pattern, certainly a credit to Portland. It is a dainty pattern quite different from other products from the Portland factory.

The following list may not be complete, as new Dahlia forms keep turning up. The 7" plate is rare and much in demand. The handle of the cake plate may be either open or closed. On a rare egg cup, the pattern weaves irregularly rather than running straight around. Another unusual item is a covered pot de creme, which has a whimsical finial in the form of a gherkin type pickle. A gherkin finial also adorns a relatively rare square sugar with a front panel showing a full Dahlia plant rather than the usual single blossom.

Forms Found In Dahlia

- † covered butter
- champagne
- cordial
- lady's goblet
- † double-ended egg cup
- water pitcher
- † oval platter, grape handles
- salt shaker
- spooner
- † bulbous water pitcher

- † 9" cake plate
- † large covered compote
- wine
- † creamer
- small mug
- 7" plate
- open salt
- † flat sauce
- † sugar
- † irregular egg cup

- † cake stand
- open compote (three sizes)
- † goblet
- milk pitcher
- large mug
- 9" plate
- master salt
- † footed sauce
- † oval relish
- cup plate

† indicates forms that have been traced directly to the factory.

Rare Dahlia double egg cup.

Dirigo Pear relish dish variant. The flowers are not in the pears, as in the more common sauce dish, and the pears have stippled bands. The central leaf is a grape leaf instead of a birch leaf.

Dirigo Pear

Anyone who lives in Maine—or has any connection with the state—would recognize the name of this pattern. Dirigo, the Latin word for "I lead," is the state motto. The reason for this pattern's use of a pear is not known. The great pity is that very few forms exist in this charming pattern. The quality of the glass is exceptional. It is very clear, resulting in a product of great beauty. To date, the only forms identified are three totally different relish dishes and sauce dishes in two sizes.

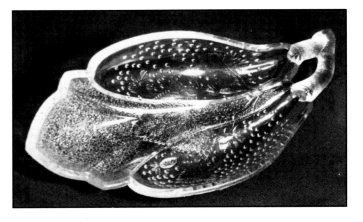

LEFT: This Dirigo Pear relish dish is shaped somewhat like the sauce dish but the pears are replaced with an unidentified fruit.

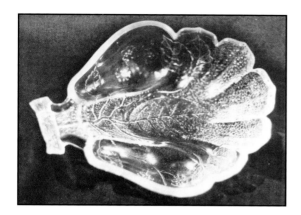

Dirigo Pear sauce dish. Note clear pears with tiny flowers, birch leaf center, and the stippling that resembles the Tree of Life pattern.

The sauce dish is shaped at one end like the Tree of Life leaf sauce dish. The other end is in the form of a tree branch from which seven smaller branches fan out into the center. The two outside branches each end in a large pear, forming the edges of the sauce. These two pears are the major design feature. The next two branches each sport a single small leaf and three small flowers. These flower sprigs overlay the clear pears. The subsequent pair of branches is longer, extending along the inside of the pear and culminating in one leaf near the base of the pear. The final branch leads to a large leaf that covers the central portion of the sauce. The background is finely stippled.

One relish dish is similar to a double sauce, with two handles. The second relish dish has two pears on one end and one pear on the other. The third has no pears, but rather two odd— and rather indeterminate— fruits. All three forms are choice and rare.

This pattern is not popular among collectors, but that probably can be attributed to the limited number of forms. It deserves better treatment from collectors; it is a fine addition to the pattern line of the Portland factory.

Birch Leaf

Birch leaf is more of a specialty item than a pattern, as there are only two forms, a large leaf and a small leaf. The form is just as the name suggests, and it is found in a large number of colors, including pale yellow, canary, vaseline, many shades of green, even more shades of blue, light amber, dark amber, and aqua. Red has been reported as a color. The pattern also was made in both white and blue milk glass. The small leaf is 6" long and the large leaf is 11".

The small sauce has been reproduced many times, but it has never been reproduced in color, and the glass of the reproduction is not of the same color as the original. Also, the reproduction does not have as prominent a midrib as the original, so there should be little confusion.

The Portland factory also produced a pattern called Leaf, for which there is only a meager description. It has an allover pattern of birch leaves. It seems that this is probably the pattern that is today known as Birch Leaf. It is an unproven pattern that is most likely Portland; it has not been attributed to any other factory.

Oak Leaf Band and Oak Leaf Medallion

These are typical Portland patterns, and they were probably Portland exclusives. These patterns do not seem to have had wide distribution, as they usually are found only in

Large medium-blue Birch Leaf; small leaves in medium and light blue.

northern New England. All forms come in two distinct versions. Originally they had two names, but in recent times, the name Oak Leaf Band has been applied to both designs. This name referred to the design that consists of a simple band of oak leaves with tiny acorns. The second version, originally named Oak Leaf Medallion, has the identical band of oak leaves, but the body of the piece below the band is stippled and divided into three sections by an elongated, stylized oak leaf, which partially conceals the mold marks. In the center of each section is a medallion, which has a reverse scallop of tiny beading. The medallion is clear except for a sprig of oak leaves and acorns.

A collection of either one of these patterns is very striking and well worth the search. It is made of fine-quality flint glass with an oily feel. The stem is nine sided and flares to the clear, round base. In most (but not all) pieces, the stem is twisted slightly.

There is no more beautiful piece of glass than the Oak Leaf Medallion covered compote. Everything about it is perfect—the shape, the quality and color of the glass,

Forms In Which Oak Leaf Band and Oak Leaf Medallion May Be Found

10" covered compote	goblet	footed sauce
13½" covered compote	wine	flat sauce
footed bowl	water pitcher	sugar
creamer	spooner	butter dish
egg cup	pickle dish	lamp
punch cup	footed punch bowl	

Oak Leaf Medallion goblet.

Oak Leaf Band goblet with prisms on bottom.

even the handsome acorn finial. It is irresistible to collectors.

Even though the number of forms is somewhat limited, a set of Oak Band or Oak Leaf Medallion is most impressive. Many of the larger forms in both patterns may have a row of round ornaments.

Forms In Which Acorn Band Is Found

goblet	creamer	sugar
sauce	spooner	footed salt
water pitcher	tall covered compote	footed bowl
open compote (three sizes)	berry dish	covered butter
wine	cordial	relish
celery vase	*cheese dish with squirrel finial	

* The squirrel finial on the cheese dish is the same as the Squirrel salt, except that the creature is holding an acorn.

Acorn Band

The oak tree seems to have held a fascination for the designers at the Portland factory. According to his descendants, Augustas Griffin, a glassblower, liked this pattern so much that he became its first collector. Acorn Band, although closely related to Oak Leaf Band, is actually quite different. Instead of having a line above and below the oak pattern, it has an open, free-form band with just a suggestion of a line at the top. In this pattern the acorns are much more prominent and look like real acorns. Strangely enough, the oak leaves are larger and more realistic. There are two distinct versions of this pattern: one has the pattern straight around the piece and the other has a wavy band that dips quite low in places. The bowl of the second version narrows more at the base. Both have hexagonal stems that flare at the clear base. The pattern is deeply sculptured in bright, clear glass with a nice ring.

Acorn Band low compote.

Acorn Band milk pitcher.

Acorn Band gentleman's goblet.

Irregular form of Acorn Band.

Chapter 10

Typical Pressed-Glass Patterns

Green water pitcher in Feather pattern.

The patterns in this chapter have the intricate designs that are so typical of pressed glass and made it particularly popular. Often they were made to rival the brilliance of cut glass, but this brilliance is produced in quite different ways. For example, in the Chain group, beading produced the effect, while in Festoon, sharp angular triangles are combined with hobnails and beads. Then there are patterns such as Loop and Jewel, which uses stippling to produce a matte effect. Many of these patterns also have rayed base patterns, which are considered another Portland signature.

The pressed-glass patterns in this chapter are Loop and Jewel, Festoon, Pequot, Fine Cut and Block, Globe and Star, Feather, Shell and Jewel, Jacob's Ladder, Roman Rosette, Good Luck, Jewel, Chain, Chain and Star, Chain and Shield, Paris, Waterford, Grape and Festoon, Tape Measure, Powder and Shot, Shell and Tassel, and Leverne.

Loop and Jewel

Even though this pattern is widely known as Loop and Dart with Round Ornaments, we are using the original factory name of Loop and Jewel. At one time, it was known as Portland, and sometimes it still is called that. There are several other patterns that make up what usually is referred to as the Loop and Dart group. There has always been great confusion about where they were made, and early writers refused to credit any of the group to Portland.

All doubts about the origins disappeare when the design patent was found to hav been issued to William O. Davis of Portlan Maine. In addition to Davis's signature, th patent application contained the signature c William H. Clifford, the patent lawyer fo Portland Glass and son-in-law of compan president John Bundy Brown. How many c the associated patterns were made at Portlan is not known. The only ones definitely trace to the factory are Loop and Heart and Loo and Jewel with Diamond Ornaments, both c which were purchased at the factory by Portland family.

Loop and Heart lamp (a prototype of Loop and Jewel).

Private Collection

Loop and Jewel covered butter dish.

90

Covered compote with double Loop and Jewel pattern.

Loop and Heart is a very different pattern that has no real reason to be considered a loop pattern, since it has no loop. The pattern consists of intersecting arches that touch at the ends, forming points. Below the alternate points is a heart. The only form in this pattern that has come to our attention is an oil lamp, which is quite lovely. The standard is made up of fluted columns, and there is a row of beading around the base.

It seems evident that the loop designs were tried out in the lamp form prior to the decision as to which pattern to patent and put into production. The lamp is also the only form of Loop and Jewel with Diamond Ornaments that we can be sure was made at Portland. We know that the pattern with diamonds was made in several places, including Sandwich

and Pittsburgh. There is also a Loop and Jewel without Ornament, which we suspect was made as part of the original lamp group, although there is, as yet, no proof of this. We do not believe that Leaf and Dart was part of this group. Rather, we suspect that it was created at Sandwich to compete with the very popular Loop and Jewel.

Indeed, Loop and Jewel was second only to Tree of Life in popularity. Like Tree of Life, it was made in many forms, but apparently never in color. The glass itself is of exceptional quality and is usually (although not always) flint. The pattern is delicate and lacy, on a finely stippled background. The stemware has a hexagonal stem and a clear base. Some of the larger pieces and plates have a double pattern.

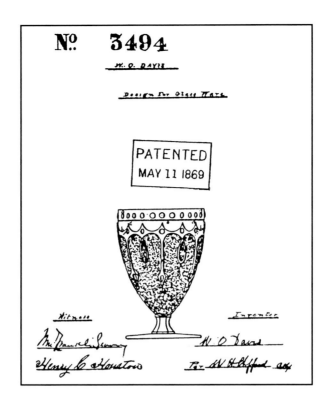

No. 3494

W. O. DAVIS

Design for Glass Ware

PATENTED
MAY 11 1869

Witness

Inventor

United States Patent Office.

WILLIAM O. DAVIS, OF PORTLAND, MAINE.

Design No. 3,494, dated May 11, 1869.

DESIGN FOR GLASS-WARE.

The Schedule referred to in these Letters Patent and making part of the same.

To all whom it may concern:

Be it known that I, WILLIAM O. DAVIS, of Portland, in the county of Cumberland, and State of Maine, have originated and invented a new and useful Design for Glass-Ware; and I hereby declare the following to be a full, clear, and exact description thereof, which will enable others to make and use the same, reference being had to the accompanying drawings, forming part of this specification, in which is shown a side view of a goblet or glass with my design illustrated thereon.

My invention relates to designs for the exterior of glass vessels of any kind, and is composed of the following forms and figures, and the arrangement thereof:

First. Around the glass vessel, where the design begins, there is a horizontal row of bosses or globular figures, *a*, projecting from the face of the vessel. Below this is a horizontal line or lines, *c*, passing around the vessel. A slight space is left between the lines and the bosses.

The top portion of the next part of the design is formed of curves, *b*, coming together, and forming the points *d*.

Between the curves *b* and points *d* and lines *c* there is a clear space of the glass of the vessel, (see *e*,) and the curves and points *b d* are formed by having the glass project slightly from the clear space *e*.

Immediately below the points *d* are circular recesses, *f*, the bottom of which may be worked into a roughened or frosted state, similar to *i*.

Below the curves *b* are other curves, *h*, bending downward.

Instead of the points *d*, however, there are seen two figures; first, the long loop *j*, formed by a raised vein or cord of glass upon the surface of the vessel; then the vein or cord *k*, having an arrow, or diamond-shaped end, *m*, with a recess in the said head, the bottom of which may be frosted similar to *i*.

The residue of the surface of the vessel is corrugated, roughened, or frosted, as seen at *i*.

The loops and the arrows are projections of clear glass upon the frosted surface *i*.

The bosses *a* may be made upon a raised rim around the vessel, represented by the lines *o*.

What I claim as my invention, and desire to secure by Letters Patent, is—

The design for glass-ware herein set forth.

WILLIAM O. DAVIS.

Witnesses:
WM. H. CLIFFORD,
HENRY O. HOUSTON.

Loop and Jewel patent application.
Courtesy of U.S. Patent Office

The actual pattern is best described by William O. Davis in the patent application, (patent number 3494, issued May 11, 1869). There is reason to believe that production of the pattern began in early 1868. Patents were slow to be issued, but they were effective as soon as application was made.

The covered sugar comes in two forms. One has a cover that fits inside, while the other has a cover that fits over the outside.

Forms In Which Loop and Jewel May Be Found

gentleman's goblet
cordial
honey
8" plate
double egg cup
covered butter
water pitcher
footed salt
9" oval bowl
10" covered compote
9" open compote
lamp, one piece, clear
finger bowl
sauce, star base
toothpick

lady's goblet
footed tumbler
sauce
9" plate
covered sugar
celery
milk pitcher
7" oval bowl
8" covered compote
7" open compote
11" open compote
lamp, brass base (signed)
cheese dish
butter pat
chamber stick

wine
flat tumbler
6" plate
single egg cup
creamer
spooner
footed master salt
8" oval bowl
9" covered compote
8" open compote
lamp, milk glass base
hand lamp
cup plate
open sugar

Loop and Jewel hand lamp.

Loop and Jewel goblet.

Festoon

This pattern (as far as we can determine, made only at Portland) is a brilliantly sparkling design reminiscent of the fairyland world that follows an ice storm. This was the first Portland pattern we collected, and we now have enough pieces to set a table with it. The set is particularly spectacular at Christmas on a red velvet tablecloth. The design is made in a wide range of forms that can be combined in many useful and interesting ways. The three sizes of cake stand, for example, can be placed one atop the other to form a three-tiered server.

Although heavily ornamented, the pattern itself is basically simple. It is best demonstrated with a plate. At the center is a typical Portland rayed pattern. You can see a four-pointed star if you mark off four equal sections of the circumference of the well of the plate. These four points are connected with festoons that curve inward almost to the rayed pattern, consisting of graduated hobs on the underside, forming a four-pointed star. Using the points halfway between the star

points, construct another four-pointed sta[r] using graduated rectangles. You now have th[e] basic central pattern of an eight-pointed sta[r]. The only other design element in this sectio[n] of the plate is a giant hob between each of th[e] star points. The ends of the hobs are cut o[ff] and then hollowed out to create feet for th[e] plate. All of the design elements are on th[e] underside of the plate, and the background i[s] finely stippled.

The flange of the plate is covered with [a] border design consisting of a rickrack patter[n] made up of small hobs with a slightly large[r] hob at each point. There is a fan decoratio[n] alternating with the rickrack. The outer edge i[s] ringed with typical Portland round ornament[s]. The glass itself, while not flint, is of fin[e] quality with great brilliance. Most of the form[s] are quite heavy. The asterisk indicates item[s] that carry much higher prices than expecte[d] considering the general prices for the pattern.

There are three variations of the sauce dis[h] that differ only in the base design. The fir[st] has only a simple star in the base, with [a] rayed medallion in the center; the second i[s]

Festoon plate.

Festoon marmalade jar.

mbellished with fans between the star points; nd the third has exactly the same pattern as 1e second except that the bottom of the 1uce, instead of being perfectly flat as in the ther forms, is dome-shaped. Not only is the 1ird variation the prettiest of the three, but it . by far the most expensive. Two additional rms, a goblet and a decanter, have been 1mored to exist, but we have never seen 1em and can find no proof of their existence.

Rare Festoon compote.

Forms In Which Festoon May Be Found

sugar
butter dish*
9½" cake stand
8" plate*
water pitcher
flat sauce (three forms)
finger bowl*
creamer

7½" cake stand
compote*
9" plate*
7½" plate*
tumbler
domed sauce
rectangular dishes (nest of three)
marmalade jar

8½" cake stand
7" plate*
water tray
berry dish (two types)
relish (oval)
spooner

Pequot

It is strange that one of the very finest of the 1rtland patterns has existed for a long time obscurity. All previous writers on the 1bject of Portland Glass have given this ·sign little recognition, even though it is one those rare patterns that, as far as we know, 1s never made elsewhere. It is also a superb-1ality flint glass in most instances (like all 1rtland flint patterns, it was not always flint), 1d it was the choice of one of the company rectors for a second pattern (the first was ·ee of Life) for his daughter. Her 1anddaughter still owns the set.

'erhaps the strangest aspect of this pattern its name, Pequot. Why should a Portland 1ttern be named after an Indian tribe from 1nnecticut? It is true that the Pequots were a uthern New England tribe, but they were a rt of the Algonquian Federation, as were the

Sapphire Pequot footed bowl. (Colors are very rare in Pequot pattern.)

Pequot covered compote.

Pequot goblet in deep amber.

Penobscot, Passamaquoddy, Micmac, an
Abenaki tribes, which we associate with Main
In fact, there were Pequots in Maine, and the
were closely allied with the Passamaquodd
Perhaps it was felt wiser to name a glas
pattern after a lesser-known tribe. Or maybe
just sounded better than the more familia
Indian names. The Pequots were fierc
warriors, which is perhaps why their help wa
enlisted by the Passamaquoddies to fight th
white settlers. Many a raid on white settl
ments involved the Pequots.[1]

The design of Pequot is made up of pointe
ovals arranged in a row with sides touchin
Over this is placed another identical row
ovals shifted to the side by the width of ha
an oval. This produces the effect of havir
intersecting ovals on top of each other, wi
smaller ovals formed by the intersection.
the point of each large oval is a sunburs
with a smaller sunburst in the lower poir
The rim of most forms is beautiful
scalloped, and the standards of the goble
and compotes are hexagonal.

Pequot is perhaps the most graceful and o
of the most elegant patterns made by tl
Portland Glass Company. A table set wi
Pequot on a dark cloth is breathtaking.

Small open Pequot compote.

Unfortunately, there are a few forms missing, so it is impossible to make a complete set, yet there are enough forms to keep the collector busy and to make a magnificent showing. With diligence, you may still expect to find most of the forms in the list below. The butter is very large and looks like a covered footed bowl.

Forms In Which Pequot May Be Found

wine	champagne	water goblet
buttermilk goblet	lady's goblet	sugar
open compote (three sizes)	covered compote (two sizes)	creamer
covered footed butter	flat butter	oval relish
oval bowls (two sizes)	footed bowls (three sizes)	celery
flat sauce	footed sauce	spooner
tumbler	marmalade	oval tray
toothpick	open salt	

Fine Cut and Block

Fine Cut and Block is one of the most avidly collected of glass patterns. Unfortunately, there is not a great deal of it, even though it was also made in the 1880's by King Glass Company of Pittsburgh. Occasionally, a piece will be found with the King signature. The soap dish is the most frequently signed item.

The pattern was made in two distinct versions, one of which collectors often refer to as Fine Cut and Hexagonal Block and the other as Fine Cut and Diamond Block. Neither of these two names seem to be used in the literature, but we will use them here for the purpose of clarity. What they were called at the factory is not known.

It is apparent that Fine Cut and Hexagonal Block was made first.[2] All indications are that it was a Portland exclusive, and only the diamond pattern was made by King Glass. The pattern is an allover pressed design that has the look of cut glass. The nature of the pattern makes it impossible to describe clearly. It is best to examine the photographs for clues to identification. In general terms, however, it consists of a pattern well known as Fine Cut that was made in many places with occasional rows of hexagons inserted. It looks a lot like the more famous Daisy and Button. The glass is quite thick and the edges of most forms are beautifully scalloped or pinked. The colors available are amber, aqua, sapphire blue, and green. The clear glass also comes flashed with color, including yellow and blue, perhaps others, although these are the only two we have encountered.

Fine Cut and Diamond Block is identical, except that the block is diamond-shaped and the glass is much thinner. (The heavy glass punch bowl is an exception.) The rims, instead of being scalloped, have a sawtooth pattern formed by the top row of diamonds. The colors found are green, sapphire blue, amber, aqua, and cobalt. The colors used for flashing the blocks are more extensive and include green, yellow, amber, blue, maiden's blush, pink, and orange. (Apparently the orange sometimes was overfired, producing a strange brown color.) Some of the flashing is somewhat opaque and shows brush marks, most evident in pink, blue, and green. Once in a while, you may find colored glass (most often amber) that has also been flashed.

Fine Cut and Hexagonal Block sauce.

Authors' collection includes such Fine Cut and Block items as: egg cup, marmalade jar, milk pitcher, compote, water pitcher, covered sugar, gentleman's goblet, champagne, footed sauces, small wine, lady's goblet, and handled berry bowl.

Rare Fine Cut and Block fan dish with loop handle.

Small punch bowl (also called orange bowl) in Fine Cut and Block.

Occasionally, we find flashed glass that was not fired after decoration, thus causing the color to wear off or chip easily.

It should be noted that there are several other patterns that use the Fine Cut and Block design (both diamond and hexagonal) in some way as panels or inserts. Where these patterns were made, or whether in fact any were made at Portland, is unknown. Given the fact that they were always trying out

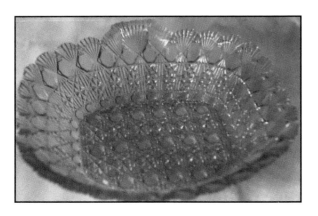

Berry bowl in Fine Cut and Hexagonal Block.

combinations of patterns or variations, it is not unlikely that some of these variations are actually Portland. They could have been prototypes from which Fine Cut and Block was extracted—much as Tree of Life was developed from Tree of Life With Sprig.

Forms In Which Fine Cut and Hexagonal Block May Be Found

† handled berry bowl
† round sauce
† cake stand

† handled sauce
† handled individual salt
† sugar

† round berry bowl
† water pitcher
† creamer

† **This pattern has been reproduced in heavy glass and garish colors. Reproductions are easy to spot!**

An assortment of Fine Cut and Block tumblers.
Swischer Collection

Fine Cut and Block spooner, often mistaken for an open sugar.

Rare green-flashed sugar, creamer, and punch cups in Fine Cut & Block.
Swischer Collection

Fine Cut and Block water pitchers with pink, blue, and yellow flashing.
Swischer Collection

Yellow (amber) flashed Fine Cut and Block group: four sizes of compotes, flat sauce, berry bowl, cracker tray.

Swischer Collection

Pink-flashed Fine Cut and Block group: covered butter, two sizes of footed sauce, finger bowl, open salt, two sizes of wines, tumbler, pitcher, creamer.

Swischer Collection

Blue-flashed Fine Cut and Block group: footed bowl, three flat bowls (with hexagonal blocks), cake stand, covered sugar.

Swischer Collection

Forms In Which Fine Cut and Diamond Block May Be Found

6" bowl
† 9" bowl
8" flared bowl
† 12" cake stand
† cordial
† water goblet
† small wine
† egg cup
† tall lamp
punch bowl and tray
† milk pitcher
7" plate
† individual salt
ruffled jelly compote
spooner
scallop-shell salt
scallop-shell dish, ring handle

† 7" bowl
10" bowl
10" flared bowl
† champagne
† buttermilk goblet
† lady's goblet
compote (seven sizes)
† finger bowl
† night lamp
perfume bottle (five sizes)
† water pitcher
12" plate
master salt
† open sugar bowl
soap dish (King Glass)
soap dish (unsigned)
powder jar

8" bowl
6" flared bowl
8" cake stand
† claret
† gentleman's goblet
large wine
custard cup
† handled lamp
† oversized tall lamp
pickle jar
6" plate
salt shaker
flat sauce
footed sauce
small punch bowl
† marmalade
† covered sugar

† **This pattern has been reproduced in heavy glass and garish colors. Reproductions are easy to spot!**

Globe and Star

We miss our old friend of many years who told us so much of the lore of Portland Glass.[3] She and her husband lived on an old New England farm that was a delight to visit. Friends and neighbors always entered the back door to savor the warmth and fragrance of her country kitchen. We would sit at the well-scrubbed pumpkin-pine table nibbling on her wonderful spicy molasses cookies, usually hot from the oven. The stark beauty of Shaker chairs and bench were softened somewhat by the cascading loveliness of the star-of-Bethlehem plant hanging in the sunny window. In the center of the table was a handsome Portland footed bowl. Little did we know that one day it would be a much-prized part of our collection.

Our friend's family was tied closely to the Portland Glass factory, and many were the stories she told us, adding greatly to our direct knowledge of the fascinating factory. In her dining room were three huge oak china closets filled with her Portland treasures, all purchased directly from the factory or received as gifts from the factory workers. Just beyond the squeaky-clean window panes

fluttered heart-shaped lilac leaves (see photo page 5). Close by, on a delicate candle stand, a Loop and Heart lamp reminded us of how often Portland Glass took its themes from nature. The windowsills were crowded with colored Portland Glass, casting jewel-like spots of light in a rainbow of colors on the white damask tablecloth. Every piece had a fascinating history, and we would remain enthralled for hours at a time.

Globe and Star footed bowl, side view.

Knowing of our interest and research, she introduced us to many other people who had Portland Glass family heirlooms. It was via this route that we were able to piece together the lineage of many of the patterns.

This dear friend provided us with our first knowledge of the existence of a previously unknown pattern, Globe and Star. We later found it in other collections, but it was the beautiful bowl on the kitchen table that we saw first. She told us how her grandfather walked to the Portland factory during a blizzard to buy his young wife the bowl as a Valentine gift.

Not only has Globe and Star not been recognized as a Portland pattern, but it seldom appears in books on pressed-glass—probably because it is so seldom found. The specimens seem to turn up mostly in northern New England, leading to the belief that it may have been made only at Portland. It just may be one of the loveliest, most extraordinary patterns to come to light.

Globe and Star is light and airy, with great brilliance. The glass is of exceptional clarity, with a nice ring. The creamer is appropriate for a description, since it incorporates all of the features that make the pattern unique. The body of the creamer globular, of clear glass, and quite large, resting on a short stem that connects it to the intricately designed hollow base. Just below the rim is a flared band made up of dime-sized circles in high relief, with a faceted daisy filling each circle. The tops of the circles form the scalloped rim. The lip is wide and low.

Globe and Star spooner with fern cutting.

Underside of Globe and Star footed bowl.

Globe and Star footed bowl, top view.

Globe and Star covered sugar.

By looking directly down into the bottom of the creamer, it is possible to see another of the prominent design elements. In the creamer, it is small and not too impressive, but on the larger forms, such as our footed bowl, it is spectacular. The base of the design, which makes a circular medallion, is an eight-pointed star with all points touching the outer circle of the medallion. The design stops a little short of the center, where the stem is attached. The arms of the star are filled with ridges and beading that give the impression of open fans with the handle at the outer edge. The triangle between the points of the star (the fans) is filled with a sunburst.

The base is quite intricate. There is a flat portion of it from which a half-inch collar rises and slopes inward. This is entirely covered with a band of circles with enclosed flowers identical to those on the rim band. The flat base is made up of four half circles with a ropelike band at the outside edge. The inner circle is filled with fanlike cutting. Between each circular section is a fan.

As though all this were not enough, there is one more design feature, and it sets Globe and Star apart from all other pressed-glass patterns that we have seen. It is the applied handle. At first glance, it may appear to be just another applied handle, but close examination reveals that it is not solid glass. It has three hollow channels running through its entire length and twisting along the way.

Globe and Star creamer. Note handle with twisted hollow channels.

Globe and Star covered butter.

Occasionally, Globe and Star will be found with one of the variations of Etched Fern or even Cut Fern decorating the clear portion of the design. This is particularly effective on the creamer and the sugar. Etched Band also was occasionally used on the clear part.

The forms in which Globe and Star may be found include sugar, creamer, two footed bowls, spooner, celery, jelly compote, two high compotes, 9" covered compote, cake stand, footed sauce, and small covered low compote. Occasional pieces may be found in light amber and light blue.

Feather

This is one pattern that, although made first at Portland, was indeed made also in Indiana in large quantity. Indiana did not claim any of the colored Feather products, however. Other names attributed to the pattern are Indiana Swirl, Doric, and Fine Cut and Feather.

A plate best illustrates his design. Its center is a medallion in the form of a twelve petaled flower. (The Indiana product has only ten petals.) The feathers for which the pattern was named form a graceful swirl around the medallion. The small ends of the feathers point toward the center, and the feathers curve gracefully outward, so that the rounded ends create the scalloped edge of the plate. Alternate feathers are different. The first type is a clear feather with a sort of beaded quill running up its center. The other type is filled with diamond-shaped figures, themselves

Feather creamer and covered sugar.

Feather cruet.

Feather plate.

made up of smaller diamonds. The overall effect is brilliant and striking. The large plate is perhaps the most outstanding form.

This pattern does come in several colors. The solid deep green glass is lovely, especially whe[n] used with clear or the very rare amber form. Some forms are the clear feather flashed wi[th] yellow, or a very deep maiden's blush.

Forms In Which Feather May Be Found

8" plate	† 10" plate	† 8½" cake stand
† 11" cake stand	† sugar	† creamer
† covered butter	compote (three sizes)	† covered compote
† goblet	† wine	buttermilk goblet
† cruet	† milk pitcher	water pitcher
† tumbler	flat bowl (three sizes)	7½" footed bowl
8½" footed bowl	toothpick	† marmalade
celery	† jelly compote	egg cup

† indicates forms that have been traced directly to the factory.

Amber-flashed Feather compote, top view.

Amber-flashed Feather compote, side view.

Shell and Jewel

In Shell and Jewel we have one of the most disputed patterns in all the annals of pressed-glass history. Who designed it? Who made it?

It is true that this pattern was made in great quantity under the name Victor by the Westmoreland Glass Company of Grapeville, Pennsylvania. It is not true, as claimed by Charles H. West, founder of Westmoreland, that it was originated by his company and brought out in 1893. The 1893 Westmorelan[d] catalog does indeed show an extensive line o[f] this pattern, which was produced in clea[r] and dark green.

A statement by Ruth Webb Lee—one of th[e] best-known experts on the subject of presse[d] glass—illustrates the folly of being to[o] positive when saying a pattern was made onl[y] in one place: "Collectors may rest assure[d] that the Victor was produced exclusively b[y] Mr. West's company, twenty years after th[e]

ortland Glass Company had
osed down. But to those who
ave no desire to acknowledge
uthful facts, the Shell and Jewel
ay still be Portland Glass."[4] Both
est and Lee believed what they
id was true! They simply did not
ave all the facts.

If, as West and Lee have stated,
ell and Jewel were produced at
estmoreland only in clear and
een, what is the explanation for
l the other wonderful colors with
stly superior quality? If you find
or-quality Victor (we will call the
ferior glass by its proper name),
u can be sure it is the Grapeville
oduct, which was a premium-
pe product intended for sale to
e grocery store trade as a con-
iner for prepared mustard.
estmoreland also made a later
oduct of iridescent colored
rnival glass, and that is indeed ugly.

This same pattern also was produced
Canada.

For those who do indeed seek the
uth, the fact is that this pattern
iginated at the Portland Glass
ompany and was made later by
estmoreland Glass Company and
hers—and claimed as their own. Since
e pattern was never patented, there
as nothing to stop them. Certainly,
enty years after the Portland factory
d closed, nobody from that company
uld be expected to object!

Frank Swan first established Shell and
ewel as a Portland pattern. It was later
onfirmed by Marion Dana. We have also
aced it to the factory via an extensive set
urchased at the showroom by a Cape
izabeth family in 1865 as a Christmas gift.
he set was clear glass with the jewels
stom-flashed in maiden's blush (cran-
rry). Occasionally, a piece of this gorgeous
t turns up.

Shell and Jewel, as produced at the Portland
ctory, must be considered superior to any
her company's production. The stippling is
ry fine, and the jewels stand out almost like
arbles protruding from the surface of the
ass. In the bowls, they create the scalloped
m. In other pieces, such as the tumbler,

Shell and Jewel bowl.

Shell and Jewel tumblers: peacock blue, amber, sapphire blue, dark green.

there is a clear rim above the jewels. Below the jewel border is the shell design, which has a flower in the center much like the rosette of Roman Rosette. On the Portland product, the mold marks are prominent.

At Portland, Shell and Jewel was made in clear, cobalt blue, very pale blue, sapphire blue, pale aqua, brilliant aqua, apple green, deep green, light amber, very dark amber, pale straw, and ruby red. A table set with clear and mixed colors is extraordinary.

To paraphrase Ruth Webb Lee: Collectors may rest assured that Shell and Jewel was designed and originated exclusively by the Portland Glass Company. To those who desire to acknowledge the facts, the Shell and Jewel is still and will ever be Portland Glass.

Shell And Jewel Forms Known To Have Been Made At Portland

water pitcher

tumbler

creamer

bowl (two sizes)

cake stand

water bottle

milk pitcher

goblet

spooner

sauce

8½" plate

cider pitcher

wine

covered butter

compote

flat cake plate

Jacob's Ladder

In Jacob's Ladder we have a pattern known to have been made prior to the establishment of the Portland Glass Company. We suspect that it was designed by Enoch Egginton while he was still working in Pittsburgh and that he brought the molds with him when he moved to Portland. We do know that the very first glass produced at Portland was made from molds that belonged to Egginton.

We also know, as mentioned in an earlier chapter, that samples of the Jacob's Ladder pattern were given to factory visitors on opening day. We have examined some of these pieces, and they are of inferior glass, green in color with many bubbles. Obviously, these were made during trial runs before opening day, while the equipment was being tested and prepared. It is also obvious that any inherent problems were solved quickly

Jacob's Ladder sugar and creamer.

Forms Found In Jacob's Ladder Is Found

6" round bowl	butter dish	candlesticks
open compote (four sizes)	covered compote (four sizes)	cordial
goblet		† creamer
oval relish	marmalade jar	mug
milk pitcher	pickle jar	† water pitcher
† flat sauce (three sizes)	6" plate	footed salt
† syrup pitcher, pewter top	† footed sauce	spooner
handled tumbler	† sugar bowl	† tumbler
† cruet	11" cake stand	celery
wine	dolphin compote	master salt
epergne (cranberry)	punch cup	punch bowl

ndicates forms that have been traced directly to the factory.

cause on opening day the factory was
oducing blown-glass the equal of any-thing
would produce in its ten-year history. Some
the opening-day products are exquisite.

he Jacob's Ladder pattern consists of clear,
ism-like panels alternating with panels of
tice work. This part of the pattern meets
e clear top band in a zigzag pattern of
angles. Stemmed forms have a nicely
eted hexagonal knob in the upper part of
e stem that flares to the clear base. Covered
ms have a finial in the form of a Maltese
oss, hence an alternate name for the
ttern—Maltese.

he pattern is known to have been made by
yce Walker & Co. in Pittsburgh in the
70's. Amber and yellow pieces occa-sionally
e found, as well as small items in bubbly
le green. The list of forms available is
ensive.

he epergne listed as cranberry (maiden's
ish color) actually is flashed clear glass. It
flashed in the prisms only and set in a
ver holder. We have not seen this item
thout the flashing, but it may exist.

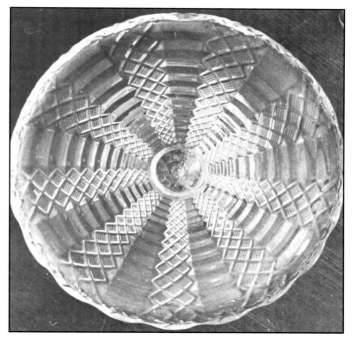

Jacob's Ladder cake stand, top view.

Roman Rosette

his is another pattern that was not made
fore Portland produced it, but was produced
tensively later. Because we have found no
rlier references from other factories, we
sume that Roman Rosette originated at
rtland Glass, where it was made in clear
ss as well as clear flashed with ruby, blue,
d amber. It was made in 1875 by Bryce,
lker & Company probably with Portland
lds.[5] A reissue produced in 1892 by U.S.

Glass (successor to Bryce, Walker) has only
fair quality. A second reissue, of poor quality,
was made in 1898. There is no indication that
any colored form was made anywhere except
Portland. The quality of the Bryce, Walker
product is excellent, and it cannot be distinguished from the Portland product. If you
want to be sure it is Portland, buy only the
colored version. The set is extensive.

The creamer in Roman Rosette is unusual in
a few respects. With most patterns, the rim

Roman Rosette blue wine mug.

Roman Rosette ruby red-flashed creamer. (Bottom flashing is very rare.)

design does not extend to the pouring lip, but in Roman Rosette it does. The rim is scalloped, with the scallop width conforming to the width of the vertical ribs of the top band. The creamer is cylindrical, tapering toward the bottom then flaring to form the domed base. The handle is molded and ornate, consisting of a teardrop pattern on each side, touching in the middle. On the water pitcher, where the top of the hand meets the body, it is clear, probably to crea a finger rest. The main body of the pitcher finely stippled with a band of clear rosett When flashed with color, only the centers the rosettes and the top band are flashe (The creamer illustrated is a unique exam in which there is flashing around t bottom.)

Forms In Which Roman Rosette Is Found

† bowl (four sizes)
† 10" cake stand
† cordial
† open compote (five sizes)
† 4" flat sauce
† relish
  tankard
  8" plate
† molasses jar (quart)
  salt/pepper, in holder
† tumbler
† goblet
† cruet

† butter dish
† caster (salt, pepper, mustard)
† wine
  covered compote (three sizes)
† footed sauce
† milk pitcher
  oval bread tray (9"x11")
  oval bowl (three sizes)
† molasses jar (pt., nickel top)
† syrup (pewter top)
† egg cup
† water tray
  cologne bottle

† 9" cake stand
† celery vase
† creamer
  square honey, covered
† child's water pitcher
† water pitcher
† 7" plate
† 4½" flat sauce
† spooner
† sugar bowl
  mug (three sizes)
† decanter (pint)

† **indicates forms that have been traced directly to the factory.**

Good Luck

As is so often the case, this is a pattern for which we can find no record of production prior to Portland, but it was made by Adams Company in the early 1880's. Since there is no perceptible difference in the pieces we have seen, we believe the Adams firm used the Portland molds. The pattern apparently was created at Portland Glass.

This is a striking pattern that deserves more of a following than it has. The design has three main elements: a horseshoe, a Persian carpet, and sprigs of leaves and flowers. Individual forms may exhibit only one of these motifs or two or all three (hence the design's alternate names of Prayer Rug and Horseshoe). Many a collector has failed to recognize the sauce dish, which has only the leaves and flowers. The goblet, one of the daintiest and most appealing made at the factory, has no horseshoe. The salts have only the horseshoe. Most of the large forms have all three elements. Round ornaments are present on many forms. Stemware may have round or knobbed stems and clear bases.

The total pattern consists of a Persian rug with the horseshoe superimposed on it and sprays of leaves and five-petaled flowers. The small leaves are much like those found in Horsehead Medallion and Grape and Festoon.

Good Luck spooner without horseshoe motif.

Finials are in the form of horseshoes. The background is stippled on some forms. Most forms are clear glass, but rare ones can be found in apple green.

Good Luck footed bowl. Note that there is no horseshoe. Round ornaments appear at top and around the base collar. Bottom and top of base have design much like Roman Rosette.

Two-handle bread tray in Good Luck pattern. All design elements appear here.

Forms In Which Good Luck May Be Found

† footed bowl
† 9" cake stand
   cheese dish
† gentleman's goblet (knob)
   gentleman's goblet (plain)
   pickle dish
   plate (four sizes)
† round master salt (rare)
† bread tray (two handles)
   bread tray (one handle)
   low cake stand (three sizes)
   deep sauce

† butter with flat lid
† 11" cake stand
† covered compote
   dish 5" x 6"
   lady's goblet
† water pitcher
   individual salt
† footed sauce
† covered sugar
   wine
† 7" low covered compote
   oval platter (three sizes)

† butter with collared lid
† celery vase
† open compote
† creamer
   marmalade jar
† milk pitcher
   master salt
   flat sauce
   spooner
   finger bowl
   cordial (rare)
† cider pitcher

† indicates forms that have been traced directly to the factory.

Jewel

This pattern has a great many alternate names, among which are Cane Column, Paneled Cane, Flower-Paneled Cane, Cane and Star, and Cane and Rosette. Why it is necessary to give so many names to a single pattern is impossible to understand. Although the oldest name appears to be Paneled Cane, there is no indication that this name was given to it at the factory. Since we have no knowledge of what it was called at the factory,

we will continue to call it Jewel, as in previou writings on Portland Glass. The name is mo appropriate, as it is a pattern collected b Margaret Jewell, one of the early researchers Portland Glass. The pattern is quite pleasin and simple, consisting of alternate vertic panels of clear glass and panels of decoratio that looks like the woven cane seat of a cha Most forms have clear rims—which often a scalloped—and clear bases. Most of th stemware has straight, round stems, th exception being the compotes, which have a knob at midstem. A variation of the basic pattern has a rayed design—sometimes referred to as a star—in the center of the plain panel. Colored forms of Jewel are not common, but the pattern sometimes is found in light amber, pale blue, cobalt, canary, or even apple green.

We have not been able to attribute this dainty pattern to any other company, so we assume that Portland Glass was its sole producer. Although there are several large collections of the design, it is not one that has caught the fancy of many collectors. As a result, it is not as difficult to find as some of the other patterns.

Jewel pattern group: sugar, covered butter, compote, spooner with star.

Covered compote with star in Jewel pattern.

Creamer without star in Jewel pattern.

Forms In Which Jewel May Be Found

flat sauce	footed sauce	creamer
covered sugar	covered butter	spooner
water pitcher	milk pitcher	lemonade pitcher
open compote (three sizes)	covered compote (two sizes)	pickle caster
celery vase	wine	cordial
champagne	open sugar	cake stand

Chain/Chain and Star

These two patterns are so much alike that they often are considered variants of the same pattern. Every form that was made in one pattern was made in the other. The Chain motif consists of a band of large circles (not touching) with a chain superimposed over them. The chain is filled with diamond quilting, and the exposed portions of the circles are rayed. The stem is round and has a wafer pattern near the base which is clear. In Chain and Star, the large circle is missing. Instead, there is a small circle between each two chain links. Above and below the chain band is a curved line that touches the link at its center and comes to a point above and below the circle. Small rays outside these lines above and below the chain links complete the design. The stem is round but

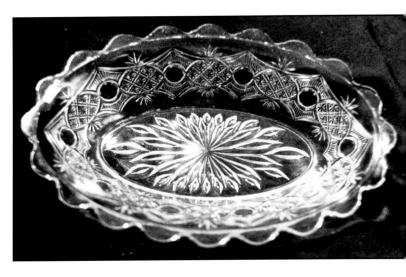

Chain and Star relish.

flares to the base, which is clear. Because of the confusion that exist in identifying these two patterns, a line drawing accompanies each of the photographs.

Details of Chain pattern and Chain and Star pattern.

Chain goblet.

Forms Found In Both Patterns

bread plate
goblet
10½" cake stand
covered compote (high & low)
sauce (footed and flat)
wine

covered butter
covered sugar
creamer
water pitcher
spooner
cordial

9⅛" compote
footed bowl (two sizes)
pickle dish
salt and pepper
open sugar
7" plate

Chain and Shield

Like the rest of the Chain group of patterns, this is a handsome design that has been more or less overlooked by glass collectors. These patterns deserve more attention because they are among the few that we can almost certainly say were never made anywhere except Portland, Maine (based on the small number of forms and the small quantity of examples found). All three are of superb-quality glass and are well designed, with enough forms to make an interesting collection.

Chain and Shield is the most spectacular of the Chain group, and its most outstanding form is the oval platter—a good piece for identification. Examining the platter from its center to the outside edge, you will see first a large sunburst on a stippled background. Within it are random snowdrops, like those of the Snow Drop pattern. Surrounding this is a row of brilliant round jewels—formed by a row of closely set hobnails on the

Chain and Shield creamer with prominent mold mark.

Oval platter in Chain and Shield pattern.

underside, which in turn form feet for the platter. The next row of the pattern is the chain, which—unlike the other chain patterns—is a rope or twisted chain with miniature hobnails forming the core of the fibers. The final row of the pattern is the ring of shields, filled with vertical lines and with their points toward the center.

The goblet in this pattern is exceptionall lovely, with a fine reeded stem. The sauce dis is very delicate and lacy looking, even thoug it is made of heavy glass. There is a single ro of beading around the rim and the piece sit up proudly on oversized hobnails. There ar fewer forms in Chain and Shield than in th other Chain patterns, but they are all lovely.

Forms In Which Chain and Shield Is Found

cordial
sugar
12" oval platter
water pitcher

goblet
spooner
compote
   (open and covered)

creamer
sauce
butter

Paris

This is another Portland pattern that was reproduced in the early 1900's by Higbee and New Martinsville. Their price for a cake stand in 1900 was only twenty-five cents. Today it would bring much more than that, even though it differs from the Portland version and is definitely of inferior quality. It should

also be noted that the prices charged at th Portland factory were very much in line wit this. Portland Glass was not expensive.

Paris—named for the town of Paris, Maine— is a very pleasing pattern and perhaps mos popular of all with first-time purchasers o Portland Glass. (Alternate names for it ar Roughneck, Victory, and Zipper Cross.) Th

Paris bowl.

Paris celery vase.

design consists of wide vertical panels separated by narrow panels cut crosswise, forming little triangular prisms. In the Portland version (but not the reproduction), alternate rows of prisms have a mold mark running through the center of them. This pattern stops from one to two inches below the rim, and a groove extends from the top of the narrow panel to the rim. At the bottom of the upper section are two prismatic rings, which extend around the piece. Above these are two short parallel cuts that cross the vertical groove. The rim has pinked scallops, which alternate with triangles located at the top of the vertical groove. The bottom of most forms is rayed with the typical Portland pattern; this is not present in the reproduction. Often the rims were bent while still hot to produce interesting shapes.

Paris mug.

Paris compote. Unusual rim was created by bending glass while it was still hot.

Forms In Which Paris Is Found

† celery vase
  7" square plate
  wine
† water pitcher
† creamer
† cruet
† mug

† 7" round plate
  cake plate
† cake stand (three sizes)
† tumblers
† spooner
  7½" deep bowl
  3" rose bowl

† 8" round plate
  salt and pepper shaker
† child's cake stand
† sugar
† butter
  goblet
  sugar shaker

low bowl (four sizes, many rim treatments)
jelly compote (many sizes, many rim treatments)
banana stand (much sought after)

† **indicates forms that have been traced directly to the factory.**

Waterford

Waterford is another pattern that, as far as we know, was made only at the Portland Glass Company. Through the years, it has become known as Sunburst, but the factory name was Waterford. It was named for the town of Waterford, Maine, not for the Irish crystal, which it somewhat resembles.[6] Evidently writers on the subject of patterned glass thought it would be confused with the Irish glass and so gave it the alternate name. The name Flattened Diamond and Sunburst has shown up recently, probably because there is still another pattern named Sunburst. According to our stated policy, we will use the original name.

The pattern is a simple one, consisting of bands of large diamonds filled with smaller diamonds. A rayed pattern fills in the space between the diamonds above and below the band. The pattern comes in clear and amber glass of high brilliance. The round bread plate comes in clear and clear flashed with amber.

The sugar and creamer are perhaps the most appealing forms in this pattern. The creamer is footed and has an elegant look. It is tall and slender, with a beautiful applied handle. The sugar is cylindrical and slightly smaller than the equally handsome marmalade jar. Each has a delightful finial in the shape of a sunflower. All three forms may be found in silver holders.

"Little Amelia's Play Set" in Waterford pattern: creamer, butter, and sugar. A spooner was also made.

Waterford bread tray. Sometimes the words are flashed yellow.

Forms In Which Waterford Is Found

† butter dish
celery
wine
† spooner
† water pitcher
† relish
† handled sauce
open compote (four sizes)

† miniature butter dish
† miniature sugar
† miniature creamer
† miniature spooner
bread plate
† individual salt
† round sauce
† covered compote (two sizes)

† sugar
† creamer
† egg cup
† goblet
plate (three sizes)
† master salt
† lamp
† tumbler

† **indicates forms that have been traced directly to the factory.**

Grape and Festoon

This is one of the more confusing glass patterns; it was made in seven variants.[7] The pattern probably originated in Sandwich where it was made with a clear background. At Portland Glass, it was definitely produced with a stippled background, and at least two variants had a clear background. An alternate name for the pattern is Stippled Grape and Festoon. The seven variants are:

1. Background stippled; grape leaf clear
2. Background stippled; grape leaf veined and lightly stippled
3. Background clear; grape leaf clear
4. Background clear; grape leaf stippled and veined
5. Background clear; grape leaf frosted
6. Background clear; shield in place of grape leaf; bunch of grapes hangs below the festoon instead of hanging from high point of festoon as in other variants.
7. Background clear; leaves of festoon point up.

Beaded Grape Medallion is apparently part of this group. We do know that the table set in flint was made in Portland.

Grape and Festoon sugar, side view—Variant 2.

Grape and Festoon goblets: Variants 7, 2, and 4.

The variants known to have been produced at Portland are 1, 2, 5, 6, and 7 and the other forms also may have been produced there, but we have not been able to find proof of that.

The basic pattern consists of a festoon of tiny leaves that dips down in three places. When the background is stippled, these leaves are in high relief.) Above the festoon, in each dip, is a large grape leaf with a bunch of grapes hanging from it. There is a wide, clear margin above the design. The items have anywhere from six to ten sides and flare to the clear base. The finial is an acorn, with an empty acorn cap on end beside it—certainly typical of Portland Glass. The identical finial was used on Honeycomb and on Tape Measure. Type 3 does not have the acorn finial; it has a six-sided knob. This variant is believed to be the original, introduced at Sandwich.

It is not certain if the Portland versions were produced elsewhere. Because of the scarcity of surviving examples, we suspect that they were not. The forms produced seem to be the same in all seven varieties. Variants 1 and 2 are of slightly thicker glass and often are flint. These are perhaps the most distinctive versions, as the pattern shows up best against the stippled background. The stippled glass is the most avidly sought after and, consequently, is more expensive. All seven variants are fine-quality glass, clear and brilliant.

Grape and Festoon covered sugar, front view—Variant 2.

Forms In Which Grape and Festoon May Be Found

† butter dish
celery vase
open compote (four sizes)
9" covered compote
† lady's goblet
flat sauce
mug
† covered sugar
water tray

† open sugar
open footed bowl
egg cup
† 10" covered compote
cordial
† spooner
6" plate
footed salt
† creamer

† covered footed bowl
gentleman's goblet
water pitcher
wine
double egg cup
oval pickle dish
tumbler

† indicates forms that have been traced directly to the factory.

Tape Measure

Of all the patterns in Portland Glass, this one probably is the poorest-quality glass. It is seldom clear, usually having a lot of bubbles, and is made of soda-lime glass of average thickness. The color varies greatly, from a bluish tint to gray or even green. The pattern, also called Shields, is known to have been used by at least one Portland-area merchant as a premium packaged with sugar.[8]

The most important design feature is, of course, the tape-measure band around the upper body. The design of the lower body consists of sets of five vertical ribs capped by an inverted chevron. Between each two sections of ribs is a more prominent rib that extends up as high as the point of the chevron. Footed forms have typical sided stems. Covered pieces are handsome, with acorn finials identical to those on Grape and Festoon.

Forms encountered include a goblet, sugar, spooner, creamer, butter, compote, sauce, bowl, and water pitcher.

Tape Measure goblet.

Tape Measure covered butter. Finial is identical to those used on Honeycomb and on Grape and Festoon.

Powder and Shot spooner, covered sugar, and creamer.

Powder and Shot

This pattern, popular with gentlemen collectors, was made at Portland and Sandwich. No other makers are known. It is an interesting pattern consisting of a powder horn with shot pouring from the open end. The horn is clear, being outlined with beading and the background is finely stippled. The stem of the goblet is nine-sided and the base is flat. On the underside (occasionally on the top side) of the base is a row of chain outlined with the same heading as used on the horn. The space inside the chain is clear, but the background is stippled. The clear area beneath the rim is exceptionally deep. The glass is of fine quality and often, but not always, flint. Pieces with applied handles have an unusual diamond impression on the bottom tab.

There apparently are no colored pieces in this pattern. The list of forms is not extensive, and the pieces tend to be rather expensive.

Powder and Shot goblet showing bowl design.

Base design of Powder and Shot goblet.

Powder and Shot open compote, top view.

Forms In Which Powder and Shot Is Found

covered butter	caster set	celery vase
covered footed bowl	covered compote	creamer
sugar	egg cup	footed salt
double egg cup	goblet	spooner
buttermilk goblet	water pitcher	sauce

Shell and Tassel

The success of the Tree of Life pattern led directly to the creation of the most vehemently contested pattern made at Portland Glass, Shell and Tassel.[9] This is one of the cases where too much emphasis has been placed on the design patent. That this pattern was patented by Augustas H. Heisey while he was employed by George Duncan & Sons in July 1881 is certain. This in no way proves, however, that the pattern was created at that time—only that no one contested the patent. Certainly eight years after the closing of the Portland factory, there was no challenge from Maine. (As we mentioned earlier, much time always elapsed between the application for a patent and its issuance by the Patent Office. Just as surely, the creator of Shell and Tassel, William O. Davis, who went to work for Duncan even before the Portland factory closed, was not likely to object if his supervisor patented one of his designs. The Shell and Tassel oval bowl and a compote may be ound with the name "Duncan" in the Tree of Life portion of the design—in the same way that the name "Davis" had been used on Tree of Life at Portland years earlier. This is without question the work of Davis, who took the design with him from Portland, along with the Portland molds.

This pattern was the last one designed by Davis at Portland Glass; when he left, he took the molds as payment for what the company owed him. The pattern has, on numerous occasions, been traced to the Portland factory. Not only was it made there, but it was made in large quantities, and there are indications that all of the colored versions probably were produced at Portland. Among the colors we have seen are yellow, light amber, deep amber, orange, light blue, dark blue, pale aqua, apple green and red. Occasional pieces with the etched Fern design used in clear areas also are certainly Portland products.

This is an extremely variable pattern, and it can be difficult to identify because the tassel is not always present. It is not uncommon to have Shell and Tassel misidentified as Tree of Life. Confusion also derives from the fact that there are two distinct forms of the pattern—one square and one round. The round version was not produced by Duncan, nor is there any other attribution, so it may be safe to assume that it was made only at Portland. It may well have been a prototype for the square form. In addition, the square form comes with the shells in Tree of Life and the rest clear, or vice versa, with clear shells and Tree of Life covering the rest of the piece. There is no indication that the form with the clear shells ever was made at Portland, and it was made only in small quantity by Duncan. Duncan catalogs indicate that the pattern was not made in as many forms there.

To describe the pattern, we will use the square form, as it is most often found and the easiest to describe. The most prominent design element is the scallop shell, located at each rounded corner of the square. It has rayed ribbing and is completely covered with the Tree of Life design. On the straight sides between the shells is a fringed drape. On two of them (opposites), there are tassels. Footed pieces usually have only two shells on the base with the drape between, but no tassel.

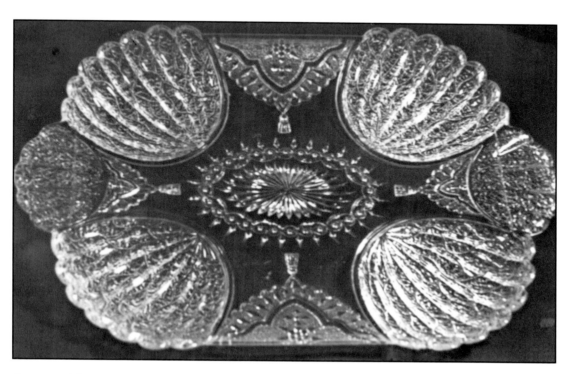

Large oblong tray in Shell and Tassel. This form best illustrates all of the design elements.

The goblet, which has been reproduced, is rare and found only in the round form, with three shells separated by drapes with tassels. The base has the typical two-shell design. The spooner, water pitcher, celery, and mugs in all sizes are almost completely covered with the Tree of Life design. Covered pieces which have shell finials, are very attractive and hard to find. The 7" vase with fer etching is very delicate and lovely. In the lis below, asterisks indicate forms we believ were Portland exclusives.

Forms In Which Shell and Tassel May Be Found

† butter dish
† 6" child's cake stand*
   covered compote (3 sizes)
   6" x 11" oval bowl
† jam jar*
† water pitcher
† open sugar
   large oval platter
† spooner
† footed sauce
† round butter dish*

   cake stand (3 sizes)
   open compote (3 sizes)
† master salt*
† individual salt
† butter pat*
† milk pitcher*
† creamer
   small oval platter
   large oblong tray
† flat handled sauce
† round sugar, dog finial*

† celery vase
† jelly compote
   9" x 10" oval bowl
   goblet
† covered butter
† covered sugar
† 7" vase*
   salt shaker
   small tray
† round berry dish*
† 8" plate (rare)

† indicates forms that have been traced directly to the factory.

Orange oval bowl in Shell and Tassel. This same color sometimes is found in Tree of Life.

Medium amber oval bowl in Shell and Tassel pattern. This form is often found in a silver holder.

Leverne

This pattern is perhaps the most delicate and lacy of all the Portland designs. The overall effect is very much like the well-known lacy Sandwich. An alternate name is Star in Honeycomb. Bryce Bros. (formerly Bryce, Walker & Co.) of Pittsburgh also made it in the 1880's. Evidently it originated at Portland, for we find no prior mentions of it elsewhere.

The pattern consists of a band of hexagons touching point to point, with a star in the center. The background is made up of tiny diamonds, which give a stippled effect. Below the hexagon (or honeycomb band) is a ban of alternating wide and narrow petals. Th wide petals are filled with a diamond patter while the narrow petals are filled wit horizontal lines. Above the honeycomb ban is a dainty drape. Some forms have a wid clear margin at the top. Most rims ar scalloped, as are most of the clear base. Stems are hexagonal. Applied handles ar exceptionally fine. We have seen no color i this pattern.

Forms In Which Leverne May Be Found

† butter dish
goblet
† 11" cake stand
flat sauce
open sugar
individual salt
6" plate
† cologne bottle

† 7" covered compote
open compote (4 sizes)
† creamer
† spooner
† tumbler
wine
celery vase
† 9" covered compote

† 9" cake stand
† water pitcher
† covered sugar
† footed master salt
8" bowl
† cruet

† indicates forms that have been traced directly to the factory.

Leverne water pitcher.

Leverne group: creamer, spooner, covered sugar, and celery.

Leverne cologne bottle and cruet.

Chapter 11

Frosted-Glass Patterns

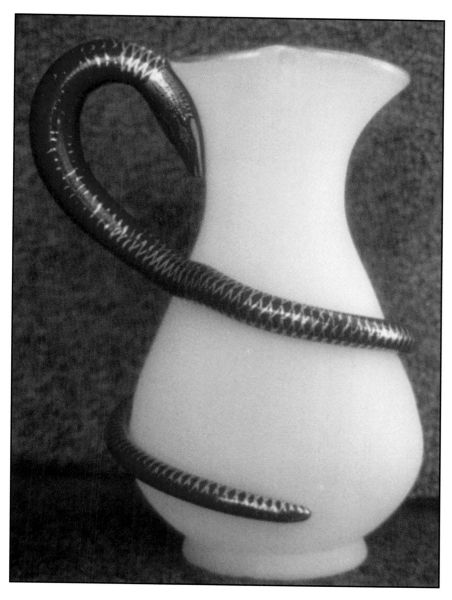

White Opaline water pitcher with cobalt blue applied snake handle.

The title of this chapter tells all—or does it? The patterns here are related by having all or part of the glass frosted. They differ, however, in how they got that way. Frosted patterns were acid finished, sandblasted, or acid etched.

Acid-finished glass is produced by exposing the glass to gaseous hydrofluoric acid to produce an allover frost. Or the glass can be immersed in a solution containing 1,000 parts water, 250 parts double fluoride of hydrogen and potassium, 250 parts hydrochloric acid, and 140 parts potassium sulfate. This latter method frosts only the portion of the glass that comes in contact with the solution. Sandblasted glass has a coarser surface and is produced by abrasives applied with compressed air. (A stencil-type mask protects areas that are to remain clear.) Acid etching is accomplished by applying a fluoride cream to the surface of the glass. After a few minutes, it is washed off, and the frosted pattern remains.

Acid-finishing patterns are Classic, Opaline, Sebago, Hobnail, and Greek Key (small items). Sandblasted patterns are Magnet and Grape, Frosted Leaf, and Greek Key (large items). Acid-etched patterns are Etched Fern and Cumberland. (Patterns described in other chapters that occasionally are acid etched are Globe and Star, Casco, Honeycomb, and Shell and Tassel.)

Classic

Without any doubt, this acid-finished design is one of the most contested patterns to appear in this book. Glass expert Ruth Webb Lee, in her writings, has attributed this pattern to Gillinder & Sons of Philadelphia. Her assertions are based on conversations with Mrs. James Gillinder, a direct descendant of the founder of the company. Lee also claims as proof the fact that the warrior plate is often found signed "Jacobus." Jacobus was the last name of a glass designer at the Gillinder factory in the 1880's who was responsible for the Westward Ho and Lion patterns. We do not dispute the fact that the pattern was made at Gillinder, but we do maintain that it was created not by Gillinder but by Enoch Egginton twenty years earlier in Portland, Maine.[1]

Water set in Classic pattern.

As produced at Portland Glass, this pattern was elegant, and it is one that is particularly prized by collectors today. Many of the forms were supported on log feet, which lent an air of distinction to the pattern. We suspect that when the Portland Glass factory closed, the Gillinder firm obtained the molds and used them years later. Gillinder immediately found that the log feet made the pieces somewhat unstable and were broken easily so the collared form of the pattern was designed by Jacobus. The plate signed "Jacobus"—as well as the Cleveland and the Blaine-Hendricks-Logan plates—was designed and made at the Gillinder factory. Of four plate designs, the only one made at Portland is the classic figure as seen on the other forms.

There can be no doubt the Classic pattern was made at Portland. It is very much in line with Victorian taste. All design elements are in high relief. The bowl of the goblet is straight sided, narrowing only slightly at the base. Six panels are separated by round columns, which support the pointed-arch tops of the panels. In alternate panels are classical figures—sometimes on a frosted

Two frosted-glass panels of Classic footed bowl.

Classic footed bowl.

background, sometimes not. The other panels are filled with a pattern that looks much like a hexagonal form of Fine Cut Block. The stem is a typical Portland tree trunk. Acorns and oak leaves are also used as decoration, such as in the finial of the beautiful covered pudding dish.

This pattern was not made in color but was of exceptional-quality flint glass. (The Gillinder product was not flint.) In the following list, an asterisk indicates the form has log feet.

Three frosted-glass panels of Classic footed spooner.

Forms Found In Classic

- † sugar*
- † butter*
- † spooner*
- † pitcher*
- † covered pudding dish*

- covered compote
- plate
- † creamer*
- † celery*
- † bowl*

- † sauce*
- wine
- goblet

† indicates forms that have been traced directly to the factory.
* indicates the form has log feet.

Opaline

Undoubtedly, there were other types of acid or satin-finished glass made at the Portland factory, but we are certain of only three: the long established Hobnail with amber (yellow) rim (also known as Francisware) and two newly identified patterns, one we have named Sebago and the second, Opaline, discussed here.

Opaline glass was very popular in the mid-nineteenth century, and a great deal of it was imported to the United States from Europe. It was generally rather heavy, with a matte surface, and it lacked transparency. The Portland version of it was very much like its European cousin, yet they do not look the same when viewed side by side. The Portland product was of exceptional quality and apparently always had a gilded edge, which was cut and polished to give an elegant look to the glass. After examining a few pieces of Portland's Opaline pattern, it is very easy to distinguish it from all other Opalines. (Although Opaline is listed and referred to as a pattern, it is actually a type of glass and can be found in many shapes.)

Perhaps the most distinctive characteristics are the beautiful lines of the forms themselves. The edges of most of them are handsomely scalloped; and nowhere is this more evident than in the magnificent punch bowl and its underplate.[1] Another outstanding characteristic is the exquisite range of colors. White is the most common, but there is an aquamarine that looks as if it had been scooped from the Atlantic, plus a lovely shade of lemon and pink that defies description. Occasionally, you will come across items that boast snakes like those in the Ophidian pattern. The serpents that are used on white glass come in cobalt blue, emerald green, and ruby red. The serpents on pink and aqua glass usually are white,

although occasionally emerald ones appear on aqua glass. No yellow glass has been found with serpents.

One of the most unusual forms with a snake is the butter dish (sometimes called a cheese dish). As can be seen in the color photograph of the pink butter dish, the design is exceptional, with beautifully scalloped edges on the under-

Pink Opaline vase with gold rim.

Pink and white Opaline cologne bottle.

plate and lid. The lid is notched so that the handles of the base can protrude through the lid, and these handles are scalloped and even tinged with gold. The white snake handle boasts exceptionally fine goldwork.

Another feature of Opaline that is not found in other patterns is the variety in the production methods. Most of the forms were produced by pressing, but some have signs of being blown molded glass, while still others such as the white and cobalt pitcher, obviously are blown. Particularly remarkable in this piece is the beauty of form (especially the free form rim) and the superbly executed applied cobalt handle. Notice the way the snake coils completely around the pitcher then lifts its head and bites into the rim. Again the goldwork is of exceptional quality and displays a design that can be considered distinctly Portland—right down to the snake's split tongue that extends into the pitcher rim.

Other forms with a serpent are sugar, creamer, cake stand, epergne, goblet, wine, candlesticks, cologne bottles, powder jars, and

Opaline punch bowl.

hair receiver. (The dresser tray does not have the serpent, which on the powder jars looks more like a worm than a snake.

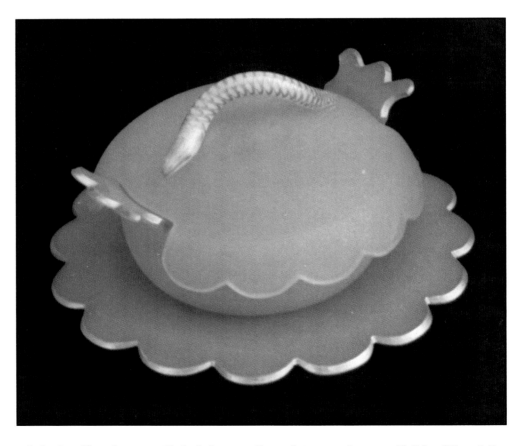

Pink Opaline butter dish (often referred to as cheese dish) with white snake and gold edge.

Forms that do not have a snake are pickle jar, plates (four sizes), tumblers, water tray, punch cups, finger bowls, butter chips, ice cream tray, platter (with handles like those on the butter dish), oval bowl, round berry bowl, sauce dishes (flat and footed), and honey dishes.

All forms found in Opaline may also be found in superb quality flint glass, often with fern cutting.

Sebago

We have long known that there was much more cut glass made at the Portland factory than has ever come to light, so it was a happy moment when we were able to trace a previously suspected, but unproven, cut (and acid-finished) pattern to the Portland factory. Since this pattern's original name seems to have been lost somewhere in time, we have taken the liberty of calling it Sebago because we found our first piece of it in an old farmhouse on the shore of the Maine lake by that name. This farm was the embodiment of old New England—stark, bare, unsoftened by any hint of shrubbery or foolishness. It seemed almost contradictory to find such an elegant example of cut glass in that setting. The owner of the lovely relish dish said that, according to her knowledge of the history of the dish, it was a wedding gift to her great-

Angled top view and side view of Sebago oval bowl.

grandmother from a worker at the Portland Glass factory, and it had been passed down through the family. Years later, a matching tumbler was found in Castine with a note in it stating, "Grandfather purchased at Portland Glass Co. auction."

As a Portland pattern, this one is unique. The basic forms are of thick, heavy glass, with very simple clean-cut lines all over the outside. A simple pattern consisting of leaves and berries was then cut through the frosting. The quality of the pieces is excellent, even though the glass is very heavy.

It is quite possible that there are many forms of this pattern that have not yet been discovered. Among the forms known to date are oval relish, tumbler, compote, oval tray, plates (two sizes), berry bowl, and sauce dishes.

Hobnail/Hobnail With Yellow Rim

The Hobnail design was made in many variations by many companies, and it is not known where the pattern originated. Apparently the Portland Glass company made Hobnail as one of its earliest patterns, since it was being sold in large quantities by two Portland retail establishments as early as 1864. One of these stores was run by Charles Jose, one of the directors of the Portland Glass Company. Steele and Hayes also stocked and sold most of the Portland patterns. It is from the records of these two stores that we are definitely able to attribute specific forms of Hobnail to the Portland factory. A few purchase orders still exist in the records of descendants of the store owners mentioned above. (It is our understanding

Francisware (Hobnail with Yellow Rim) items: water set, covered butter, toothpick, creamer, covered sugar, and open sugar.

at the records will be given to the Maine
storical Society at a future date.) It is now
town that only Hobnail with large hobs was
ade in Portland, and that it was sold in clear
ass, frosted glass with a clear rim, clear
ass with yellow-flash rim (Francisware), and
ear glass with maiden's blush rim.

Many of the Francisware forms that we
tow were made in Portland are shown in the
ccompanying photographs. They include
ater pitcher, child's pitcher, tumbler,
othpick holder, covered butter, covered
gar, open sugar, and creamer. Forms not
town are celery vase, covered compote,
overed candy jar, and dresser set (cologne
ottle, powder jar, hair receiver, and tray).

In clear glass (or frosted and clear), only
oblets have been attributed previously to
ortland. It now appears that the water set
itcher and tumblers) also was made in
osted glass with a clear rim. Everything that
as made in yellow was also made in
aiden's blush with the exception of the
resser set.

Francisware syrup with pewter top.

Francisware water pitcher and child's pitcher from play set.

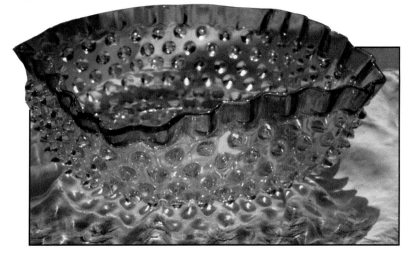

Francisware berry bowl without frosting.

Magnet and Grape

Magnet and Grape was first introduced at Sandwich and then copied by the Portland Glass Company with a minor, but all important, change—instead of a stippled pattern on the leaf, Portland sandblasted the leaf to produce a heavy frosting. Portland made the pattern in flint glass. It seems that Sandwich did not want to be outdone so they made some glass with a frosted leaf, but they simply frosted the stippled-leaf product they already were making. (Occasionally, you will see a piece of the Sandwich ware that was not frosted enough, so the stippling still shows.) The nonflint Magnet and Grape with Frosted Leaf thus can be assumed to be Sandwich Glass and the flint Portland Glass. The name at both factories was the shorter one, the descriptive addition having been made later to distinguish the two types.

The pattern consists of a large frosted grape leaf from which hangs a bunch of grapes enclosed in the magnet. This design usually is found on both sides, but some goblets were made with a shield on one side with the words, "E Pluribus Unum." Stemware was an octagonal stem with a knob at the bottom. The glass is quite heavy, with resounding ring. Prices are as hefty as the glass.

Magnet and Grape goblet with shield and words "E Pluribus Unum."

Magnet and Grape spooner showing grape-leaf panel.

Magnet and Grape spooner showing magnet panel.

Forms In Which Magnet And Grape Is Found

gentleman's goblet	lady's goblet	tumbler
wine	champagne	creamer
covered sugar	open sugar	egg cup
footed sauce	flat sauce	footed salt
covered butter	milk pitcher	water pitcher
8" covered compote	9" covered compote	9" open compote
10" open compote	footed bowl (three sizes)	celery vase
decanter (quart)	decanter (pint)	spooner
water tray	oyster plate	

Frosted Leaf

Perhaps one of the finest compliments the Portland Glass Company ever received came from an unexpected source—Ruth Webb Lee. In her writings, Lee tended to denigrate the Portland Company and its products, so it is heartening to read in *Early American Pressed Glass* (1960): "The Frosted Leaf has a charm and grace which excels many of the patterns collectible in sets. It is seen more often in Maine than other places. While it is possible to collect a set, a diligent search of the New England area is required. It is one of my favorites and graces my table more frequently than any other glass."

Just what is this pattern that so captured her fancy? It is a simple, elegant, flint pattern with a bell-like ring, and it truly deserves this

Frosted Leaf covered butter.
Frank H. Swan Collection,
Portland Museum of Art, Portland, Maine.

Frosted Leaf Lady's and Gentleman's goblets.

attention. The major design element is a serpentine band of frosted poplar leaves pointing alternately up and down. Below the band are clear vertical panels. The area above the band is clear. Finials and stoppers all have the band of frosted poplar leaves. Stems are hexagonal and flare to the clear base. The frosting of the leaf was produced by sandblasting the surface.

The most outstanding forms of the pattern are a lamp with milk glass base, beautiful decanters, and magnificent compotes. Although amethyst glass is scarce in Portland, it is the only color in which Frosted Leaf was made. However, it is rare indeed and it commands a price as much as twenty times higher in amethyst than in clear glass. The celery vase has two styles. One style has a scalloped edge and a plain base, while the other has a plain edge and starred base, with a row of pressed leaves below the band of frosted leaves. Frosted Leaf glassware is among the most difficult patterns to locate.

Frosted Leaf master salt, double egg cup, and whiskey.
Marion P. Dana Collection,
Portland Museum of Art, Portland, Maine.

Frosted Leaf quart decanter.

Marion P. Dana Collection,
Portland Museum of Art,
Portland, Maine.

Frosted Leaf lady's goblet.

Forms In Which Frosted Leaf May Be Found

covered butter dish
cordial
decanter (quart)
gentleman's goblet
water pitcher
footed master salt
sauce, star base (two sizes)
covered sugar
8" plate
lamp with milk glass base
covered compote (four sizes)

open compote (four sizes)
decanter (pint)
lady's goblet
footed tumbler
individual salt
footed sauce
ale
celery vase
champagne
creamer
egg cup

wine
flat tumbler
spooner
open sugar
7" plate
whiskey
double egg cup

Greek Key

This is a pattern that was made by many glass factories and still is being made. Each factory has always had its own variations: Sometimes the key is sandblasted, but not always. Base designs vary greatly, as do stem designs. Alternate names are Roman Key, Grecian Border, and German Key.

We know what the Portland variation of the Greek Key looked like, but we cannot be certain that no other company used the identical design. The Portland product was of fine-quality flint, with a substantial ring. (The reproduction has no ring.) The key may be frosted or not, but the stem always is hexagonal and the base is clear. The goblet comes in two forms, the most common of which has a side band of the pattern at the top of the bowl; the lower portion of the bowl is ribbed much like Scalloped Flute. The second form has a much narrower pattern at the bottom of the bowl and a narrow band of ribbing above it.

The list of forms that follows is somewhat speculative, since we do not know definitively that all of the forms were made at Portland. We do know, however, that at least 30 forms were made in the Greek Key pattern at Portland.[2]

Greek Key goblet and decanter.

Forms In Which Greek Key May Be Found

† goblet (two sizes)	wine	cordial
tumbler	† footed tumbler	sauce
berry bowl	egg cup	† covered sugar
† creamer	† covered butter	celery
† spooner	† master salt, footed	mustard pot
compote (three sizes)	plate (two sizes)	punch bowl
punch cup	† lamp	water pitcher
jam jar	relish	† decanter
milk pitcher	† epergne	

† indicates forms that have been traced directly to the factory.

Etched Fern

This is a pattern that has been overlooked by most writers on the subject of pressed glass. It is an attractive pattern that is fairly easy to find at very pleasing prices. Perhaps it is just too available. It is a good pattern to start collecting, because the prices for it are almost certain to increase sharply.

The basic forms of Etched Fern are identical to those of Cumberland, the only difference being in the graceful, feathery fern patterns which vary greatly. Evidently the design, size and placement of the fern decorations was a the whim of the artist who was doing the etching. (Some items are acid etched, while others are wheel cut.) Occasionally, you wil find a lovely piece of blown-glass with the same graceful cut designs. Fern patterns are

Etched Fern water bottle.

Two shapes of Cumberland goblets.

lso occasionally found on Globe and Star, oneycomb, or Shell and Tassel items.

Cumberland

Like Casco, which appears in the next apter, this is a simple pattern. Its alternate ame is Etched Band. The goblet in this attern comes in four different forms, parently for reasons discussed below. The st form is identical to Casco, except that it s three bands: one is about ¼" wide, while ere are fine bands ¼" above and below it. e banding is about ½" from the rim of the blet. The sizes of the band vary with the size the form. The second goblet form is a ainer version of the first. Its stem is round ther than hexagonal and forms a ring where joins the bowl. The base is a separate piece

rather crudely applied to the stem. The third form is the most distinctive. Its bowl is a straight-sided flare with etching the same as on the above two forms. The stem is rather intricate. Where it meets the bowl there is a wafer-shaped section. As the stem proceeds downward, it flares out, forming a conical shape. There are two more wafer-shaped sections just above the base. The base itself has a ring where the stem joins it. The fourth form is a marriage of the second and third versions: the bowl from the third version and the stem and base from the second version.

Although this pattern is not popular with collectors, it is quite nice in its simplicity. While we can never know for sure why there are four distinct forms of the goblet, we suspect that after the disastrous fire of 1867 at the Portland factory, it was necessary to make new molds. The third form may have been created at the time as a refinement of the fourth version. Perhaps rather than continue the second form as a separate item, the company simply etched bands on Casco, which looked enough like the second form to be used with it. The second and fourth forms are thus most likely the original Cumberland pattern. Forms that can be found include wine goblet, whiskey, cordial, tumbler, several sizes of compotes open and covered. Cumberland is occasionally found in milk glass.

Chapter 12

Unadorned Glass Patterns

**Small covered compote with red flashing in Broken
Column.**

The patterns in this chapter do not have the variety of molded surface decorations that distinguish the designs described in the preceding chapters. The patterns here depend on their shapes alone to make them outstanding, and many are indeed splendidly beautiful in their simplicity! They may or may not be flashed in color.

The group of undecorated patterns includes Portland, Banded Portland, O'Hara, Scalloped Flute (Palmer Prism), Nestor, Honeycomb, Broken Column, Falmouth, Snow Drop, Orbed Feet, and Casco.

Portland

Many collectors seem to love the simplicity of the Portland pattern (also called Plain Portland). The quality of the glass is fine, and occasionally examples are found in such colors as vaseline, green, straw, and blue.

In most forms, the pattern consists of eight wide vertical panels with arched tops that do not extend to the rim. Tracing the panel downward, you will find that it narrows and at the same time curves slowly out to a point, then reverses and curves inward, widening slightly. The panels are separated by a groove, which becomes very wide and deep at the

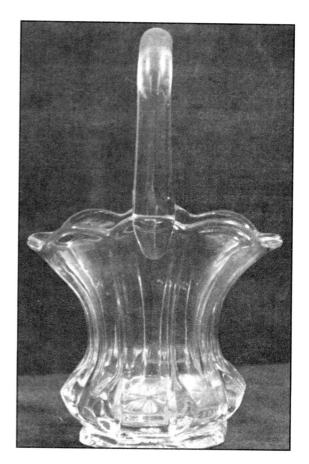

Portland basket.

Portland souvenir sauce dish.

outer point of the panel. Stemware has eight sides. The base is octagonal, with four rays on each side converging on the center. The base design in the round-base tumbler varies, with either 20 or 24 rays. There also are octagonal-based tumblers, which are only 3¾" high rather than the usual four inches. The range of forms is extensive. Compotes may be found in this pattern with a complex cover design that is scalloped in the inverse of the base so that top and bottom interlock.

Portland lamp and candlestick.

Portland punch set.

Portland items: cruet, salt shaker, toothpick and two sizes of
syrup with pewter tops.

Portland relish (in silver holder) and atomizer.

Forms In Which Portland May Be Found

sugar
covered butter
toothpick
vase (three sizes)
punch cup
compote (three sizes)
milk pitcher
covered compote (three sizes)
syrup (two sizes)
raised tumbler
plate
cologne bottle
cake stand
relish
ring tree
oval individual ice cream

creamer
wine
collared sauce
candlestick vase
punch bowl
bowl (two sizes)
salt shaker
cruet
square sauce
flat tumbler
powder box
tall lamp
decanter
5½" cereal
finger bowl
spooner

cordial
flat sauce
goblet
candlestick
water pitcher
basket
sugar shaker
lemonade pitcher
egg cup
pin tray
handled lamp
celery tray
oval olive dish
oval ice cream tray
atomizer

Banded Portland

This pattern is identical to Portland except for the diamond point band located at the midpoint of the vertical panels and the large notch flanked by two smaller notches at the point where the upper and lower panels meet. Unlike Portland, this pattern (also referred to as Virginia when it was part of a state series in the 1880's) has not been found in solid-colored glass. The only color is in the form of flashing, which may be on the bottom half of the panels, the top half of the panels, or both. The flashing may be cranberry (maiden's blush), yellow, green, blue, ruby, or gold. All of the forms found in the Portland pattern are also found in Banded Portland.

It should be noted that there are two other patterns closely related to Portland that apparently were made in limited quantity at the Portland Glass factory. Quartered Block was made in the lamp in two sizes. Evidently the pattern was tried out as a lamp (a common practice at the factory) as well as a few other forms but never made as a full set. The pattern later was expanded and made elsewhere.

Another trial pattern made in a limited number of items (including cracker jar and dresser set) was Long Buttress, which later was developed into an extensive line and produced in quantity by the Fostoria glass firm. Both Quartered Block and Long Buttress are represented in the Egginton family collection.

Banded Portland goblet.

Ruby-flashed Banded Portland berry bowl.

Banded Portland vase.

Banded Portland cider pitcher
or tankard.

Banded Portland pin tray flashed with
dark red and printed in silver.

Two green-flashed perfume bottles and maiden's blush toothpick in Banded Portland.

Banded Portland maiden's blush salt shaker.

Banded Portland covered jelly compote with plain Portland lid.

Banded Portland covered jelly compote. Note cutout for jelly spoon. Lid probably is plain Portland because band on it would detract from the band on the base.

Banded Portland butter dish with gold.

O'Hara

Like all of the other glass companies, Portland Glass had an entry in the family of loop designs. This pattern, also known as Portland Petal, was introduced by William O. Davis when he moved to Portland Glass Company from O'Hara Glass Works in Pittsburgh. Davis named the design for his former employer, James O'Hara, founder of the Pittsburgh firm and once a Quartermaster General in Mad Anthony Wayne's famous "Legion."

O'Hara can be confused very easily with other loop patterns, but there are a few distinguishing features that help with identification. The Portland product, for example, is of fine-quality flint glass with a resonant ring. The glass, like most Portland flint, is of exceptional clarity. Stemmed forms have the typical hexagonal stem. The loops are deeply pressed and gracefully shaped, somewhat more elongated than most.

The list of forms is not extensive. It includes goblet (two sizes), celery vase, covered sugar, creamer, spooner, wine, lamp, compote (three sizes), covered butter, candlestick, and salt.

O'Hara goblet.

Small O'Hara compote.

Scalloped Flute

This is Portland's mystery pattern, known t collectors as Palmer Prism, the name it wa given by Frank Swan, as a matter c convenience, at a lecture. He obviously did nc know the factory name for it and probabl never had seen a piece of the glass, for h does not discuss it in his book, nor was ther a sample of it in his master collection (whic is now the nucleus of the collection at th Portland Museum of Art).

O'Hara pitcher (very heavy, thick glass).

Joshua Sears Palmer was treasurer of the Portland Glass Company, and by some accounts the manager of the facility. He was not, however, involved with the artistic end of the business. It has long been assumed that he was the creator of this charming pattern, as his name appears on the patent issued for it on August 4, 1868. There is strong evidence that he merely applied for the patent on behalf of the company and that the true designer was William O. Davis, the creative genius of the company at the time.

One would think that it would be an easy matter to find examples of this pattern and identify it by the description given on the patent application. This is not the case, however; collectors have been searching in vain until just recently. Many similar patterns have been called Palmer Prism even though they obviously did not conform exactly to the drawing on the patent application (perhaps because many people find it difficult to recognize a glass pattern from a drawing).

Common flint compote may have been a prototype for Prism (one of twelve purchased at the factory for a Portland candy store).

For quite some time, collectors have been giving another Portland pattern the Palmer Prism designation. Prism, the factory's name for that other pattern, was made of poor-quality flint glass. It evidently was made for commercial purposes and was very inex-

Compote in Scalloped Flute pattern measures 8½" in diameter and 4⅜" high. The 2½" bowl is joined to the typical Portland hexagonal base by a wafer. The design is so sharply molded that at first glance it appears hand cut.

Private Collection

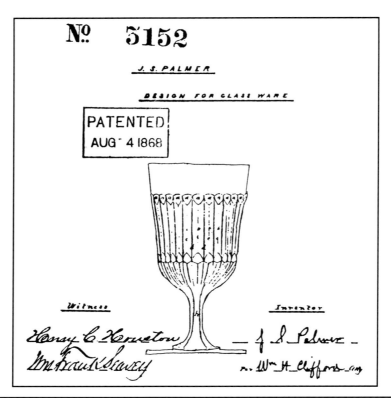

United States Patent Office.

J. S. PALMER, OF PORTLAND, MAINE.

Design No. 3,152, dated August 4, 1868.

DESIGN FOR A GOBLET.

The Schedule referred to in these Letters Patent and making part of the same.

TO ALL WHOM IT MAY CONCERN:

Be it known that I, J. S. PALMER, of Portland, in the county of Cumberland, and State of Maine, have originated and designed a new and useful Design for Glass-Ware, of which the following is a full, clear, and exact description, reference being had to the accompanying drawings, forming part of this specification, in which is shown a view of a goblet with my design thereon.

My design is composed of prisms and figures formed by indentations or depressions in the glass, having three corners, (see a,) arranged upon the surface of glass-ware, as hereinafter set forth.

First, there is arranged a row of the three-cornered figures or cuttings a a, &c., around the outer circumference of the ware, being in the form or shape illustrated in the drawings, at a.

These form hollow or curved indentations in the ware, with raised edges and sides. From these are drawn downward the prisms b, highest at the centre c, and falling off at each side, so that between each pair of prisms is a V-shaped recess or hollow, (see d.)

At the lower end of the prisms are other figures, similar to those at the upper ends of the prisms; then follows a second set of prisms, converging, if necessary, to conform to the narrowing form of the specimen of ware, or to its stem, as h.

Above the upper row of the figures marked a is the plain surface of the glass.

The figures a at the top are broadest at their upper edge, and tapering towards the bottoms. In the row of puntys at the bottom this form is reversed.

What I claim as my invention, and desire to secure by Letters Patent, is—

The design for glass-ware, as herein set forth and shown.

J. S. PALMER.

Witnesses:
WM. H. CLIFFORD,
HENRY C. HOUSTON.

Patent application for Scalloped Flute pattern.

Courtesy of U.S. Patent Office.

pensive. The Prism compote is still found frequently in Maine.

In 1987, collectors discovered genuine examples of Scalloped Flute. Perhaps the reason it did not show up earlier is that there are so many prism patterns, just to confuse the issue, and collectors were not sure of Scalloped Flute when they saw it. The photograph of the compote shows clearly that it does indeed look like the patent drawing. Made of exceptional quality flint glass with a beautiful clear ring, Scalloped Flute is a fitting reward for the diligent searcher. Items found so far are the compote, goblets in two sizes, wine, footed sauce, peg lamp, and a table lamp that is truly a gem.

The real mystery is why so little of the pattern was ever made even though it is one of only three patterns for which the company obtained a patent. Production could start as soon as the patent application was filed (protection began upon application rather than upon final approval), so the new set of molds made in August 1867 for "a new prism type pattern" must have been for scalloped flute. A month later the factory was destroyed by fire, and probably most, if not all, of the new molds were lost. Perhaps they had to concentrate their efforts on replacing the molds for the older patterns already in demand and could not afford to spend time remaking molds for a new and untested pattern. By the time they finally got to work on the Scalloped Flute pattern again, the factory's fortunes were ebbing due to labor disputes and the loss of the *Arthur Kingman*, and probably only tried–and–true patterns were kept in production. Whatever the reason, it is sad that such an exceptional pattern is so scarce.

For further reading on this interesting pattern, see The Glass Club Bulletin of the National Early American Glass Club, 151, Winter 1986/87.

Nestor

Nestor is a pattern that some collectors have long identified as Portland Glass. We now know that this pattern was made and probably originated at the Portland factory.[1] It was also made elsewhere at the turn of the century. For instance, it appeared in the 1903 Montgomery Ward catalog with this description: "Bright imperial green glass in panel design, the

Fine Cut and Block compote and Nestor sauce dish in sapphire blue.

Nestor tumbler with flat panels and no pinking. This piece is amethyst.

panels are enameled or decorated in white in a tasty manner, the pattern is a pretty design of lace work, the gold fired and very effective." For a few years during that era, Montgomery Ward commissioned one or two exclusive pressed patterns each year. These patterns seldom appeared in their catalog for more than one year.

As far as we can tell, the Portland product was never made in green. Montgomery Ward's shade of green was totally different from any Portland green. We do know that it was made at Portland in clear, blue, and lavender. Occasionally, a piece turns up with multicolor enamel, quite different from the later white decoration.

The design features six or eight (depending on the size of the form) elongated panels with rounded ends. The rim is scalloped and pinked, the base is domed, and the handles are applied.

Forms to look for in the Nestor pattern include berry bowl, sauce, sugar, creamer, spooner, butter, water pitcher, and tumbler.

Honeycomb

The Portland Glass Company is only one of a great many factories that, over the years, have produced the Honeycomb pattern in endless variations. (Among the alternate pattern names are Thousand Faces, Cincinnati, and Vernon.) Most of the pieces can be removed from consideration immediately, because we do know what the Portland product looked like. It was made in two variations that are illustrated best by the goblets. In the first type, there are four rows of honeycomb, which are smaller toward the bottom of the bowl. The stem is round and the base is clear. The second type has only two rows of honeycomb, with a panel below them. (Some people consider this an elongated third row of honeycomb.) The stem is ten-sided and flares to the clear, round base.

The Cut Fern designs on Honeycomb items can vary from piece to piece. These are just a sampling of the forms that may be found.

Honeycomb covered butter and oval covered dish. Finial is the same as used with Tape Measure pattern.

It is difficult, although possible, to find true Portland Honeycomb. However, with the huge number of glass firms involved in making the pattern, it is impossible to say with complete assurance that even a piece that conforms exactly to type was indeed made at Portland. Like Globe and Star, Honeycomb sometimes is found with the Etched Band or Etched Fern design added above the honeycomb. The glass itself varies in quality; some is even fine-quality flint. All of the forms are rather thick walled and heavy.

Honeycomb creamer.

Forms In Which Honeycomb May Be Found

- † champagne
- lady's goblet
- † covered butter
- † spooner
- † decanter
- † high compote (two sizes)
- † oval covered dish
- milk pitcher

- † cordial
- † egg cup
- † sugar
- † lamp
- † sauce dish
- low compote (two sizes)
- † berry bowl
- † cider pitcher

- † water goblet
- † double egg cup
- † creamer
- † wine
- celery vase
- † cake stand
- † water pitcher

† indicates forms that have been traced directly to the factory.

Broken Column

In this rather strange pattern, we have another design that probably originated at the Portland Glass Company. (Alternate pattern names are Rattan, Irish column, and Notched Rib.) There is no indication of how it came to be, but we can find no evidence that any other company made it before or even at the same time as Portland. It was reproduced in the 1890's by Columbia Glass Company and by U.S. Glass.[2]

It is not possible to separate the products of the different factories, because there is no great difference in the quality of the glass. Also, we do not know what specific items were made at Portland, with the exception of a few

Cobalt Broken Column punch cup.

that have been traced. These include pickle dish, cake plate, round open compote, and small square covered compote, sugar and creamer, and cobalt punch cup.

The glass is clear, brilliant, and heavy, with a waxy feel. It can be found in green and occasionally cobalt blue; it frequently is found with a clear glass flashed with ruby or gold in notches and sometimes on the rim.

It was with the Rattan pattern that Margaret Jewell started collecting Portland Glass for the Society for the Preservation of New England Antiquities in Boston. She gave it this name and was the first to trace the pattern directly back to the Portland Glass Company. (Information on her work in identifying this pattern appeared in the *New York Sun*, March 31, 1934.)

The pattern is characterized by pronounced vertical ribs that are deeply notched. The Rattan name is probably the

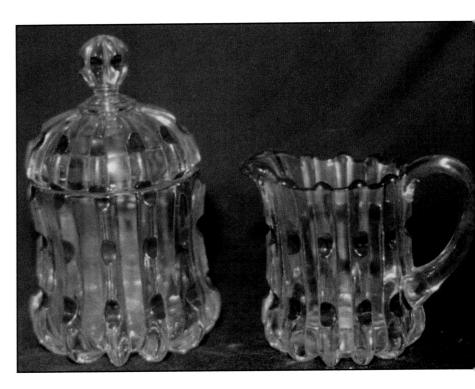

Broken Column, covered sugar, and creamer.

most apt for it. This is a widely collecte pattern, and it now is being made as museum reproduction, but the reproductio is marked clearly with the initials of th maker. The list of forms is extensive.

Forms In Which Broken Column May Be Found

goblet	tumbler	plate
sauce	† covered sugar	† creamer
spooner	rectangular bowl (two sizes)	water bottle
† open compote (three sizes)	† covered compote (three sizes)	cracker jar
covered butter	wine	marmalade
covered bowl	water pitcher	berry bowl
cruet	relish	whiskey
banana dish	basket	cake stand
celery	custard cup	finger bowl
lady's goblet	pickle caster	salt and pepper
sugar shaker	† punch cup	† cake plate

† **indicates forms that have been traced directly to the factory.**

Forms In Which Falmouth May Be Found

ale glass
champagne*
footed bowl (three sizes)
decanter/stopper (quart)*
covered bowl (three sizes)
goblet*
jelly glass
lemonade glass
pony beer
7" plate
individual salt
spooner*
water tumbler*
tumbler, tapered
claret
covered nappies, low foot

bitters bottle
9" compote*
cordial
decanter/stopper (pint)*
oval bowl (four sizes)
lady's goblet
jug (quart)
beer mug (half pint)
water pitcher*
covered preserve dish
master salt
sugar
tumbler (half pint)
wine*
butter dish
celery vase*

compote (four sizes)
creamer*
open decanter (quart)
egg cup*
3½" honey
jug (pint)
tall beer mug
6" plate
open preserve dish*
4" sauce*
tumbler (gill)
tumbler, bar taper
wine tumbler
handled egg cup

Falmouth

According to Frank Swan, several companies, including New England Glass Company and Sandwich Glass, made this simple pattern over a long period of years. (An alternate pattern name is Huber.) All of the Portland product was made in flint glass, thus eliminating most of the articles that are found most frequently. The Portland version was crystal clear, with a good ring. The goblet has ten vertical panels, each about 1" wide at the top, tapering to about ½" wide at the bottom. The stem is hexagonal, flaring to a hexagonal wafer at the top and also flaring at the base. The glass is heavy, suggesting it might have been made for hotel use. The list of forms is long, and it is impossible to determine which ones were made by which glass company. In the list above, the asterisk indicates items known to be of Portland origin.

Snow Drop

There is so little to this pattern that it is difficult to describe. The forms are simple, with an allover stipple and clear, confetti like specks scattered randomly throughout the stippling. Some forms have clear rims, and the shell sauce dish has a clear fleur-de-lis in the handle. (An alternate pattern name is Ashland.)

This is the only pattern (besides Tree of Life) that even comes close to having a signature—one complete set consisting of an ice cream

Falmouth goblet.

tray and twelve sauce dishes has been found in its original box, just as it was shipped from the factory.[3] This has put to rest for all time the detractors who have claimed this glass to have been a product of the 1890's. It is foolish to try to date glassware by its pattern; just because a given type of pattern was popular at a certain time does not mean that similar patterns could not have been produced earlier! There are no infallible rules for dating glassware. Forms in which Snow Drop may be found include goblet, wine, shell sauce (three sizes), tray (two sizes), toothpick holder, finger bowl, relish, butter dish, round bowl (three sizes), water pitcher, milk pitcher, round sauces, tumbler, compote, cake stand, plates, sugar, creamer, and spooner.

There is reason to believe that a similar pattern—called Egg in Sand or Egg in Snow—was also made at Portland. This pattern i identical to Snow Drop except for the ova edge decoration. Unlike Snow Drop, which i always clear, it is possible to find Egg in Snov in lovely colors. Most commonly found ar plates in several sizes. You may also com across goblets, tumblers, water tray, suga creamer, butter, relish, and water pitcher. I you are exceptionally lucky, you may ever find an Easter egg!

Snow Drop goblet.

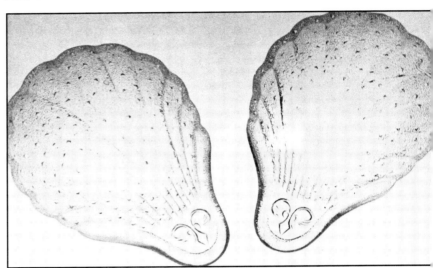

Two shell-shaped Snow Drop sauce dishes.

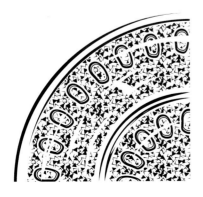

Detail of Egg in Snow Pattern.

Plate with Egg in Snow pattern, a variant o Snow Drop.

Orbed Feet items: mustard, creamer, salt, and toothpick.

Orbed Feet

This is a pattern that was discovered and named by Frank Swan in his book, *Portland Glass*. We have been unable to find any further indication (besides Swan's identification) that this strange pattern was produced at Portland. The forms are straight-sided, clear glass, with a ring of small glass balls around the base that form the feet. The number of feet depends on the size of the form. The toothpick holder has ten feet, as does the salt. The sauce has twenty feet, the berry bowl has sixty, and the tumbler has twenty-five. This is not a

Evidently Frank Swan had not seen the goblet when he named the Orbed Feet pattern.

particularly attractive pattern, and it is not one that seems typical of the output of the Portland Glass Company.

Bar Glass

In addition to the glass made for home use, we should mention a little known class of wares often referred to as Bar Glass. The factory produced a large volume of heavy glass of plain design intended for use in hotels, bars, and onboard ship.

Much of this glass is entirely unknown to us today. Until recently there have been no examples available. Even the tumbler shown by Frank Swan in his book was unavailable. Several items in the same pattern have recently surfaced and are now in the author's collection. Just another example of the collectors reward for his unending quest for the unknown. This glass is of exceptional quality flint with a truly bell-like ring and great clarity. There are surely other patterns and forms yet to be found of this elusive glass.

Two examples of Bar Glass.

Casco

Probably the simplest of all Portland patterns received a name that was very logical for a factory that overlooked beautiful Casco Bay.

A very easy pattern to identify, particularly in the goblet (the most frequently found form), Casco has a hexagonal stem that rises to a well-shaped bowl. The stem flares out to form six petals on the bottom of the bowl. If you look straight down into the bowl, you will see what looks like a lovely flower in the bottom. As the stem approaches the base, it fattens into a knob.

The six panels end in rounded petals halfway through the knob, then it constricts again before joining the base. There is a small ring where the stem joins the base.

Although this particular goblet is not as heavy as other such items, this probably is a sample of glass made for the ship, bar or hotel trade. Other forms that we have come across, in addition to two sizes of goblets, are a wine and a compote.

It seems particularly fitting that this book should end with a pattern named Casco, as Casco Bay is where it all began.

Casco

Appendix I

People Known to Have Worked at Portland Glass Company

Child Samuel cake stand (rare).

John Bundy Brown	president	1863-70	Charles Hanes	glass mold maker
	director	1863-70	Nathanial Hamlin	glassworker
Rensellaer Cram	president	1871-72	Francis T. Wood	glassworker
	director	1862-72	Charles Harris	N.A.
James H. Smith	president	1872-73	Charles Harbrook	glassworker
	director	1871-73	Elmora Huston	glasspacker
Joshua S. Palmer	treasurer	1863-69	Edward Jones	lamp maker
Albert B. Stevens	treasurer	1870-73	Daniel Kelly	glassworker
Enoch Egginton	superintendent	1863-66	Henry Lewis	window maker
James Beard	glassmaster	1863-73	William Lineham	glassmaker
	superintendent	1866-67	William Loomis	glassmaker
William O. Davis	superintendent	1867-72	James Manning	glassworker
William B. Bent	glasspacker	1866-72	Matthew Masterson	glassworker-glassblower
	superintendent	1873	Edwar McKeever	glassblower
Charles E. Jose	director	1863-73	John McKeever	glass presser
Joseph Walker	director	1863-69 & 73	John McQuade	glassworker
George Brock	director	1863-70	Joseph Merritt	glass cutter
Philip H. Brown	director	1871-73	Judy Mercer	glass decorator
John E. Donnell	director	1871-73	Timothy Looney	glass cutter
A. K. Shurtleff	director	1871-73	James H. Moore	glassworker
Charles H. Forbes	director	1871-73	William B. Wood	glassworker
Joseph Egginton	foreman cutting room		Esther Wood	lamp painter
Oliver Egginton	glassblower		Lewis F. Zoller	glassworker
Ann Baker	glasspacker		Henry M. Hadley	glass inspector
James Barbour	brassworker		Eldrige J. Hadley	glassworker
E.C. Bolles	glassblower		Emile T. Genet	glassworker
William T. Boucher	glassworker		Archibald Forsyth	glassblower
*Samuel Bowie	glassworker-glassblower		John Colson	glassworker
C.P. Brackett	watchman		William F. Russell	glassworker
Andrew J. Cash	glasspacker		Owen Sheridan	glassworker
John Connors	glassblower		John Sullivan	glassworker
Thomas Chick	glassblower		Dennis Tane	glassworker
Dennis Cole	decorative window maker		Thomas Murphy	glassworker
Emmit Drake	blower of glass novelties		John O'Brien	glassblower
Walter Fay	glassblower		Cornelius O'Brien	glassmaker
Francis J. Deechan	glassblower		Robert Quale	blacksmith
William Thorndike	glassblower		Dennis Quale	blacksmith-mold maker
Arthur Turner	glassblower		Michael Reagan	glassworker
Timothy Welch	glassblower		Robert Robson	glassblower
Michael White	glassworker		Augustas Griffin	glassblower
			Marcus Swift	N.A.

*Samuel Bowie came to the Portland Glass Company as an unskilled worker and eventually became a glassblower. When he left his native Maine he went to New Bedford, Massachusetts where he worked for the Mount Washington Glass Co. prior to forming his own company, The Mount Washington Etching Co. and later the S.R. Bowie Co. producing exceptional engraved and painted glassware. Slowly emerging information indicates that Mr. Bowie is a much more important figure in the history of American glass than previously indicated. His work can be viewed at the Glass Museum, New Bedford, Massachusetts.

Appendix II

Patterns Made at Portland Glass Company

Very rare Cut Fern creamer with the handle like the one used on Globe and Star.

Pattern	Flint	Colors	Rare	Original	Exclusive	Blown
Acorn Band	yes	no	mod	yes	yes	no
Banded Portland	no	no	mod	yes	no	no
Birch Leaf	no	yes	no	yes	repro	no
Broken Column	no	yes	no	yes	no	no
Casco	no	no	no	?	?	no
Cathedral Rose	yes	no	yes	yes	yes	yes
Chain	no	no	no	yes	yes	no
Chain and Shield	no	no	no	yes	yes	no
Chain and Star	no	no	no	yes	yes	no
Classic	yes	no	yes	yes	no	no
Crackle	some	yes	mod	no	no	some
Cumberland	no	no	no	?	?	no
Cut Fern	yes	no	no	?	?	most
Dahlia	no	yes	no	yes	no	no
Deer and Pine	no	yes	mod	yes	?	no
Dirigo Pear	no	no	mod	yes	yes	no
Egg in Snow	no	yes	no	?	?	no
Etched Fern	some	no	no	?	?	some
Falmouth	some	no	no	no	no	no
Feather	no	yes	no	yes	no	no
Festoon	no	no	mod	yes	yes	no
Fine Cut and Block	no	yes	yes	yes	no	no
Frosted Leaf	yes	no	yes	yes	yes	no
Globe and Star	no	no	yes	yes	yes	no
Good Luck	no	no	mod	yes	no	no
Grape and Festoon	some	no	yes	yes	yes	blown
Greek Key	some	no	no	no	no	no
Hobnail	no	no	no	no	no	some
Honeycomb	some	yes	no	no	no	no
Horsehead Medallion	no	milk	yes	yes	yes	no
Jacob's Ladder	no	yes	no	no	no	no
Jewel	no	yes	no	yes	?	no
Leverne	no	no	yes	yes	no	no
Loop and Jewel	most	no	no	yes	no	no
Lotus	no	no	no	yes	yes	no
Magnet and Grape	yes	yes	yes	yes	w/frost	no
Nestor	no	yes	no	yes	no	no
Oak Leaf Band	yes	no	yes	yes	yes	no
Oak Leaf Medallion	yes	no	yes	yes	yes	no
O'Hara	yes	no	mod	no	no	no
Opaline	some	yes	yes	no	no	some
Ophidian	some	yes	yes	yes	yes	some
Orbed Feet	no	no	no	no	no	no
Owl and Possum	yes	no	yes	yes	yes	no
Paris	no	no	no	yes	no	no
Pequot	yes	yes	yes	yes	yes	no
Portland	some	yes	no	yes	?	no
Portland Wreath	yes	no	yes	yes	yes	yes
Powder and Shot	yes	no	yes	yes	yes	no
Roman Rosette	no	yes	no	yes	no	no
Rose Band	yes	no	yes	yes	yes	some
Scalloped Flute	yes	no	yes	yes	yes	no

Pattern	Flint	Colors	Rare	Original	Exclusive	Blown
Sebago	yes	no	yes	yes	yes	some
Shell and Jewel	no	yes	no	yes	no	no
Shell and Tassel	some	yes	no	yes	no	no
Snow Drop	no	yes	no	yes	yes	no
Squirrel	some	no	yes	yes	yes	no
Tape Measure	no	no	no	yes	yes	no
Tree of Life	some	yes	no	yes	no	no
Tree of Life Milk Glass	no	yes	yes	yes	no	no
Tree of Life with Sprig	no	no	yes	yes	yes	no
Waterford	some	yes	no	yes	?	no
White Iris	yes	no	yes	yes	yes	yes

Patterns named by the authors are Opaline, Ophidian, Sebago, Portland Wreath, Cut Fern, Cathedral Rose, and White Iris.

Pattern	Patent	Flashed	Frosted	Cut	Enamel	Gold
Acorn Band	no	no	no	no	no	no
Banded Portland	no	yes	no	no	no	yes
Birch Leaf	no	no	milk	no	no	no
Broken Column	no	yes	no	no	no	yes
Casco	no	no	no	yes	no	no
Cathedral Rose	no	no	no	yes	no	no
Chain	no	no	no	no	no	no
Chain and Shield	no	no	no	no	no	no
Chain and Star	no	no	no	no	no	no
Classic	no	no	yes	no	no	no
Crackle	no	some	no	no	no	yes
Cumberland	no	no	yes	no	no	no
Cut Fern	no	no	no	yes	no	no
Dahlia	no	no	no	no	no	no
Deer and Pine	no	no	no	no	no	no
Dirigo Pear	no	no	no	no	no	no
Egg in Snow	no	no	no	no	no	no
Etched Fern	no	no	yes	no	no	no
Falmouth	no	no	no	no	no	no
Feather	no	yes	no	no	no	no
Festoon	no	no	no	no	no	no
Fine Cut and Block	no	yes	no	no	no	no
Frosted Leaf	no	no	yes	no	no	no
Globe and Star	no	no	some	yes	no	no
Good Luck	no	no	no	no	no	no
Grape and Festoon	no	no	no	no	no	no
Greek Key	no	no	yes	no	no	no
Hobnail	no	yes	yes	no	no	no
Honeycomb	no	no	yes	yes	no	no
Horsehead Medallion	no	no	no	no	no	no
Jacob's Ladder	no	no	no	no	no	no
Jewel	no	no	no	no	no	no
Leverne	no	no	no	no	no	no
Loop and Jewel	yes	no	no	no	no	no
Lotus	no	no	no	no	no	no
Magnet and Grape	no	no	yes	no	no	no
Nestor	no	no	no	no	yes	yes
Oak Leaf Band	no	no	no	no	no	no
Oak Leaf Medallion	no	no	no	no	no	no
O'Hara	no	no	no	no	no	no
Opaline	no	no	yes	no	some	yes
Ophidian	no	no	no	no	no	yes
Orbed Feet	no	no	no	no	no	no
Owl and Possum	no	no	no	no	no	no
Paris	no	no	no	no	no	yes
Pequot	no	no	no	no	no	no
Portland	no	no	no	no	no	yes
Portland Wreath	no	no	yes	yes	no	no
Powder and Shot	no	no	no	no	no	no
Roman Rosette	no	yes	no	no	no	yes
Rose Band	no	no	no	yes	no	no
Scalloped Flute	yes	no	no	no	no	no

Pattern	Patent	Flashed	Frosted	Cut	Enamel	Gold
Sebago	no	no	yes	yes	no	no
Shell and Jewel	no	no	no	no	no	some
Shell and Tassel	no	some	no	no	no	no
Snow Drop	no	no	no	no	no	no
Squirrel	no	no	no	no	no	no
Tape Measure	no	no	no	no	no	yes
Tree of Life	yes	no	no	no	no	yes
Tree of Life Milk Glass	no	no	no	no	yes	no
Tree of Life with Sprig	no	no	no	no	no	no
Waterford	no	yes	no	no	no	no
White Iris	no	no	no	yes	no	no

Four patterns have had their original names restored: Waterford (Sunburst), Cumberland (Etched Band), Loop and Jewel (Loop and Dart), and Scalloped Flute (Palmer Prism).

Appendix III

Stockholders in the Portland Glass Works (1870-1873)

Broken Column water bottle.

J.B. Brown
Philip Brown
Joseph Walker
Portland S. Packet Co.
Rufus E. Wood
E.W. Morton, Kennebunk, ME
John E. Donnell
R.H. Hinckley
Burges Fobes & Co.
Augustas E. Stevens & Co.
B.F. Adams, Boston, MA
William L. Putnam
A.K. Shurtleff
Jeremiah Dow
Charles Forbes
Joseph Iesley
A. & S.E. Spring
W. Davis
John Thompson, New York, NY
H.M. Hart
Lynch, Baker & Co.
Rensellaer Cram

Charles Jose
Leonard Billings
T.H. Weston
Jacob McLellan
George Dow, New York, NY
George Hunt
Myron Lyford, Waterville, ME
C.M. Rice
St. John Smith
Samuel Hanson, Buxton, ME
H.N. Jose
A.B. Stevens
W.F. Milliken
Hampshire & Baltimore Coal, Philadelphia, PA
George Brock
James D. Fessenden
G. & L.P. Warren, Westbrook, ME
H.J. Libby
William O. Davis
William Deering
George Brock

NOTE: All resided in Portland unless otherwise noted.

Appendix IV

Inventory of Portland Glass in "Lost Town"

Garden of Eden water pitcher.

48	Tree of Life sauce dishes
6	Tree of Life berry bowls
6	Tree of Life covered sugars
6	Tree of Life creamers
6	Tree of Life butters
24	Tree of Life goblets
12	Tree of Life lemonades
6	Fine Cut and Block finger lamps, assorted finishes
6	Fine Cut and Block tall lamps, clear and amber
6	Loop and Jewel finger lamps
2	Loop and Jewel lamps with milk glass bases
3	Quartered Block lamps
1	Nestor berry set, amethyst
2	Shell and Tassel cake stand (small child's size)
24	Falmouth goblets
24	Festoon tumblers
2	Festoon cake stands
4	Festoon water pitchers
12	Squirrel salts
1	Shell and Tassel red oval bowl
6	Banded Portland candlesticks, gold-flashed
4	Banded Portland butter dishes, gold-flashed
4	Banded Portland sugars, gold-flashed
4	Banded Portland creamers, gold-flashed

Appendix V

Suggestions for the Collector: Compatible Patterns

Roman Rosette creamer with red.

It is becoming increasingly difficult to collect many Portland Glass patterns in complete sets, so we are providing suggestions of patterns that coordinate well.

All patterns of the Tree of Life group may be mixed and matched at will.

Garden of Eden and Lotus, as well as decorated and undecorated Ophidian, were obviously created to be used together.

Chain, Chain and Shield, and Chain and Star were all limited patterns that work very well together.

Acorn Band, Oak Leaf Band, Oak Leaf Medallion, Squirrel, and Owl and Possum may be mixed for a pleasing set.

Plain Portland and Banded Portland, of course, can be used together. The less obvious O'Hara also works well with them.

Dahlia combines well with Snow Drop and Egg in Snow. They even come in the same colors.

Good Luck pieces without the prayer rug and horseshoe motifs work well with Deer and Pine, as does Grape and Festoon.

Feather and Fine Cut and Block are often collected together.

Paris and Jacob's Ladder make a sparkling combination.

Snow Drop and Egg in Snow may be used to fill out a collection of Powder and Shot.

The only pattern that goes well with Rose Band is Paris.

Pequot and Scalloped Flute (Palmer Prism), while very different, look good together.

Shell and Tassel has a perfect companion in Tree of Life.

We would be glad to help collectors with their questions about Portland Glass. Write to us at:

The Serena Colby Gallery
P.O. Box 900
York Harbor, ME 03911

—T.L. and L.L.

Glossary

Acid Finish: A matte surface produced by treating glass with hydrofluoric acid. The liquid form of the acid produces a transparent matte. The gaseous form of the acid—as well as many soluble fluorides—produces a matte surface of considerable opacity.

Annealing: Slow cooling of glass to prevent cracking and to create a strain-free product.

Blowpipe: A long iron pipe used by the glassblower to gather a blob of glass and blow it into a useful form.

Britannia: A metal alloy used for tableware and having the look of silver. The composition is basically copper and tin, with small amounts of antimony and sometimes bismuth.

Color: See Glass Colorants.

Crucible: A large pot made of refractory clay in which the glass is made.

Cullet: Broken glass added to the melt to help bring all the components into solution more quickly.

Cutting: A method of glass decoration producing sharply detailed designs. The cutting was done with small copper disks charged with emery and rotated at high speed. The process is often referred to as "wheel cutting." Also referred to as engraving, which is the current preferred term.

Enameled Glass: Glass decorated with powdered glass in various colors mixed with oil of lavender and applied to the surface with a brush. The glass item was then fired in a kiln so that the powdered glass melted and adhered to the surface of the object.

Engraving: See Cutting.

Flashing: A special type of enameling in which the glass used is transparent and applied thinly to the surface.

Font: The portion of an oil lamp that holds the oil.

Gaffer: A glassworker who could do almost any job in the glassworks, usually the assistant to the glassblower.

Gather: The blob of glass on the end of the blowpipe.

Glass: Material that exists in a super-cooled liquid state. Its appearance is that of a solid, but there is no crystalline structure. since the molecules have no pattern, it is a true liquid, and as such will transmit pressure and strain throughout the entire mass. The glass discussed here is essentially a mixture of the silicates of calcium and the alkalis.

Glass Colorants: This subject was covered briefly in the test but may profit from further discussion. The oldest method of coloring glass red is the use of a solution of gold in aqua regia or the use of a deep red powder known as "purple of Cassius," a mixture of gold and tin chlorides. When the glass is first cooled, it has no color, but it develops a beautiful shade of red when reheated just to the softening point. The exact shade of red is controlled by the addition of tin or silver salts, with the results ranging from light cranberry through deep ruby red to vinaceous purple. The color is caused by the fact that the gold is distributed in the liquid (glass) in a very finely divided or colloidal state, allowing only the red light to pass. Glass also can be colored red with cuprous oxide, although this method is more difficult to control. This second method was seldom used because the oxide is so easily oxidized further, in which case the glass produced would be green. A dull red may be obtained with the use of ferric oxide. Yellow glass is produced by the addition of potassium antimonate or antimony glass (a fused sulfide of antimony). Silver chloride or borate added to the melt will also produce yellows, as with some organic substances. Aloe wood placed above the crucible produced a very nice amber color due to the presence of alkali sulfates. Green is produced chiefly with cupric oxide, resulting in a brilliant emerald color. Other green tints may be obtained with chromium oxide. A dull bottle green is produced by ferrous oxide. Blue is produced by cobalt oxide. The intensity is varied by the amount of cobalt used, and the range of tints from blue to aqua can be varied by the addition of silver and organic material. Violet is obtained from the black oxide of manganese. Black glass is made by the addition of iridium sesquioxide. Addition of manganese produces what is called black amethyst. Addition of cobalt produces a blue-black glass.

Glory Hole: The vents in a glass furnace that must be kept open at all times to prevent fire or explosion.

Grog: Burned fire clay that is ground and reused.

Kerosene Ware: (also referred to as Kerosene Trade): Kerosene lamps and lamp chimneys, which were made in huge quantities.

Maver Board: A hard board of iron (or sometimes marble) used when working with hot glass.

Obsidian: A naturally occurring form of glass.

Polishing: Used to give a more finished look to the rough place where the pontil was broken off. Sometimes rim roughness or mold marks were removed by polishing.

Pontil: The point where the finished piece of blown glass is broken from the glassmakers tool, which is also called a pontil.

Sandblasting: The process of producing a matte finish on a piece of glass by bombarding it with fine sand propelled by high-pressure air.

Spooner (Spoonholder): A container used on the table to hold extra teaspoons.

Standard: The stem and base supporting a piece of glass such as a compote.

Terra Alba: Pottery made with white clay.

Chapter Notes

Chapter 1
The People and the Place

1. "Manufacturers of Portland No. 1." *Portland Transcript*, June 12, 1864.

2. "Portland Glass House." *Portland Daily Press*, May 26, 1866.

3. The information presented in the following paragraphs was compiled primarily from newspaper accounts of that era. Of special note are the *Eastern Argus* and the *Portland Transcript* (see bibliography for complete listings). An early chemistry treatise by Roscoe and Schorlemmer, also listed in the bibliography, was helpful not only as a source of information about the chemistry of glass, but also for determining proper word usage for the era. Wherever possible, we have used terms that would have been used at the Portland factory rather than the modern equivalents.

4. Our sources for the tour are newspapers of the era, most important of which are the *Eastern Argus* of April 16, 1864, and the *Portland Transcript* of June 12, 1864. Additional information came from an Egginton family diary that is still owned by a descendant, along with many interesting glass items. Like all who own valuable items, she wishes to preserve her anonymity. The diary is particularly useful because it seems to have been used by the whole family to record what they had done and what they were planning to do. Please note that the layout of the rooms in our diagram is accurate but the relative sizes are completely speculative.

5. For further reading on glassmaking, many of the books in the bibliography will be found to be helpful. Of special interest is *Treatise on Chemistry*, by Roscoe and Schorlemmer.

6. There is at present a controversy over the use of the terms *milk glass* and *opal glass*. Both have been used for many years for different degrees of the same thing: a glass rendered opaque by the addition of an insoluble white powder, usually a phosphate. There has been a movement of late to use *opal glass* universally even though traditionally it was used to designate glass with a low content of opacifier, being therefore somewhat translucent and at the same time opalescent. *Milk glass*, while not always properly applied, has been the most common term for a long period and refers to the completely opaque glass. The Portland product is almost always opaque thus we use this much more familiar term as it is also the proper one. Note that a piece with some translucence will occasionally be found.

7. The terms *cutting* and *engraving* have been used interchangeably through the years. We have used *cutting* or *cut glass* only because that is the terminology used by the Portland factory. The process used is intaglio cut, or wheel cut, which is entirely different from the familiar brilliant cut glass. This process is also called *wheel engraving*, which is the term used more frequently today.

8. The description of the sales room is from the Egginton diary (see note 4 above). The specific entry is about Mrs. Egginton's plans for decorating the room. While we cannot be sure the plans were executed there is no reason to believe otherwise.

Chapter 2
History of the Portland Glass Company

1. The biographical information on John Bundy Brown was gathered from several newspaper sources. The most important source, however, was the *Portland Board of Trade Journal* for May 1888.

2. Most of the set had been completed before Egginton came to Portland. This set was not for the White House but for a family member, as a gift.

3. For further reading on the Portland fire, see Augustas F. Moulton, *Portland by the Sea*.

4. The best description of the fire will be found in the *Portland Transcript* of September 28, 1867. Accounts will also be found in other Portland papers of the same date.

5. More information on Swan's discovery of Portland Glass will be found in "Hobby Study Makes Providence Man Authority" *Providence Sunday Journal*, November 30, 1947.

Chapter 3
The Story of a Town Lost Deep in the Woods

1. Mention of the barrels of glass was made in Marion Dana's introduction to the reprint edition of Frank Swan's *Portland Glass* and also in letters from Miss Dana to the authors.

2. The anonymous letter was in response to an advertisement we ran in a Portland newspaper requesting any available information on the Portland Glass Company or its products. This type of ad was quite productive and brought forward many people who had information.

Chapter 5
Blown-Glass and Novelties

1. Our source for information on Emmit (sic) Drake is the Egginton Family diary referred to in note 4, chapter 1.

2. The precise dates for American glass items have been the source of considerable disagreement over the years. Our preferred authority wherever a question arose was George and Helen McKearin's book, *American Glass* (see bibliography).

3. This information was based on personal interviews, telephone conversations, and correspondence with descendants, who wish to remain unidentified.

4. G.A. Emery, *Ancient City of Georgeana and Modern Town of York* (Maine) *From Its Earliest Settlement* (see bibliography).

Chapter 7
Cut Glass

1. Also known as wheel cut, or wheel engraved, glass. We have used cut glass as

it is the term used in the Egginton diary and thus is likely the term used at the factory.

Chapter 8
The Tree of Life Group:
Portland's Best-Known Pattern

1. Miss Magaret Tolman of Portland, owns a pair of hand compotes (10 inches in diameter and 10.5 inches high) purchased at the factory by her grandfather.

2. The window in the Wilson Castle was the first that could be proven to be of Portland origin. We have since seen several other windows in Portland that used the same glasses. At least two have the initials "D. C." carved in the wood frame, which probably stands for Dennis Cole, listed in the Portland City Directory as a window maker at the Portland Glass Co.

Chapter 9
Patterns from Nature

1. More information on the Squirrel pattern can be found in Ruth Webb Lee's book, *Victorian Glass*.

2. The present owners of this set have shown us the bank draft used to purchase it (as well as the Dahlia) at the factory in 1865. They are an old Portland family who wish to remain anonymous to protect their privacy.

3. In the Egginton diary (see note 4, chapter 1) which states that the pattern was too expensive to produce.

4. See note 2 above. This is in reference to the set of Dahlia purchased at the factory.

Chapter 10
Typical Pressed-Glass Patterns

1. For more information on Indians in the Americas, we suggest Brownell's fascinating book, *Indian Races of North and South America* (see bibliography).

2. The Hexagonal Block pattern was purchased in 1865 at the factory by a Portland family. They still own this extraordinarily lovely set in aquamarine blue.

3. Although this lady is deceased, the family has requested that we protect their privacy by not publishing her name.

4. R.W. Lee, *Victorian Glass* (1940).

5. R.W. Lee, *Victorian Glass* (1940).

6. The Egginton diary (see note 4, chapter 1) includes the comment, "Must come up with a design for Waterford presentation" along with a rough sketch of the pattern, which apparently was designed for some town occasion in Waterford, Maine.

7. Our information on the Grape and Festoon variants have been drawn from several sources, including the books of Ruth Webb Lee and Frank Swan (see bibliography), as well from personal observation.

8. See Marion Dana's introduction to the reprint edition of Portland Glass (listed in bibliography).

9. For further reading on Shell and Tassel, see *Hobbies* (August 1938), the books of Frank Swan, R.W. Lee, *Victorian Glass* and *Antiques* (January 1966).

Chapter 11
Frosted-Glass Pattern

1. Frank Swan fully identified this pattern, and we also have traced a purchase directly to the factory. There is no indication that the collared version was ever made at Portland.

2. A notation in the Egginton diary (see note 4, chapter 1) states, "the 30 molds for key finished at last."

Chapter 12
Unadorned Glass Patterns

1. We have traced to the factory some lovely lavender pieces in this simple pattern given as a Christmas gift by a Portland Glass factory worker and now owned by a Scarborough family.

2. Information on the Broken Column pattern can be found in Margaret Jewell's, "Rattan Pattern Glass Identified" *New York Sun*, March 31, 1934.

3. This interesting set was purchased from a Westbrook antiques dealer by Marion Dana and is now in the Portland Museum of Art. It is described in Miss Dana's introduction to the reprint edition of *Portland Glass* by Frank Swan.

Sources and Bibliography

We wish to particularly thank Mr. John Holverson, former director of the Portland Museum of Art, for allowing us full access to the correspondence files of the museum.

We are also grateful to Marion Dana, who kindly shared much of her vast knowledge of the subject with us and who was instrumental in establishing proof of several patterns, including Snow Drop, Tape Measure, and Shell and Jewell.

It is unfortunate that many sources cannot be listed because individuals are reluctant to have their privacy disturbed or are fearful for the safety of their heirlooms. We have used names only when permission has been granted; if this makes research by others more difficult, we are indeed sorry.

A diary by a member of the Egginton family has been one of our best sources. We were allowed to see it on the condition that the owner's name not be published.

Another very important source of information are the hundreds of letters we have received from all over the country in response to Mrs. Ladd's appearance on the PBS television program "Antiques."

The following institutions have been most helpful during our research: the Old Dartmouth Historical Society, New Bedford, Massachusetts; the Portland Musuem of Art and the Maine Historical Society, both in Portland, Maine; Essex Institute, Salem, Massachusetts; and Portsmouth Athenaeum, Portsmouth, New Hampshire. We often are asked where people can see Portland Glass. Following is a list of museums that have glass on display.

The Portland Museum of Art
7 Congress Square, Portland, ME
The Swan and Dana Collections are housed here. Although they have the largest collection of Portland Glass, they seldom display a great deal of it.

The Maine Historical Society
485 Congress St., Portland, ME
A rather small collection.

The Harrison Gray Otis House
Boston, MA
The Jewel Collection

Wheaton College, Norton, MA
The Raabe collection contains interesting examples of milk glass.

Chrysler Museum, Norfolk VA
Fine examples of Ophidian.

Foxcroft School, Dover-Foxcroft, ME
Some very nice colored items.

York Institute Museum
375 Main Street, Saco, ME
A nice small collection.

Portland Glass References

Newspapers

Antique Trader, August 27, 1974, (James Matthews. "Hobnail").

Antique Trader Weekly, May 25, 1976, Beverly Stoughton, ("Tree of Life: Sandwich, Portland, or Pittsburgh").

Boston Evening Transcript, February 18, 1939, ("New Light on Antique Portland Glass").

Boston Evening Transcript, February 25, 1939, ("Portland Glass Patterns").

Boston Post, March 27, 1867, (Francis Sprague).

Daily Courier (Portland), 1863-64.

Eastern Argus, August 24, 1863; May 28, 1866, July 21, 1867; September 18, 1867.

New York Sun, March 31, 1934, (Margaret Jewell. "Rattan Pattern Glass Identified").

Portland Daily Press, April 16, 1863; June 13, 1864; December 26, 1864; January 6, 1865; January 13, 1865; May 26, 1866, ("Portland Glass House").

Portland Press Herald, January 5, 1965, ("Portland Glass Purchase Inspires Collection of Glass Americana Primitives").

Portland Price Current, September 21, 1867, ("Total Destruction of Portland Glassworks").

Portland Sunday Telegram, January 28, 1934, ("Portland Glass Long Forgotten, Now Coming into Limelight as Some of Finest in Country").
—, October 2, 1938, ("Paper Tells of First Glass Factory").
—, July 6, 1941, ("Glass Factory Brought City Fame for One Decade").
—, January 2, 1949, ("Portland Glass Once Famous").
—, November 30, 1958, (Tom Ormsbee, "William O. Davis of Portland Created Famed Glass Design").

Portland Transcript, July 4, 1863, ("The Manufacture of Glass").
—, June 12, 1864, ("Manufactures of Portland No. 1").
—, December 7, 1866, ("Explosion at the Glassworks").

Portland Transcript, April 25, 1863; November 21,1863; January 9, 1864; October 28, 1865; November 25, 1865; January 20, 1866; October 17, 1866; December 1, 1866; December 15, 1866; September 28, 1867; April 25, 1868; November 28, 1868; January 29, 1870.

Portland Weekly Star, September 20, 1867, ("Another Great Fire").

Providence Sunday Journal, November 30, 1947, ("Hobby Study Makes Providence Man Authority").

Sunday Telegram (Portland), December 8, 1876, ("Portland Glass Firm Ranks with Best in Early America").

Magazines
Antiques, August 1933, (Martha York Jones, "Portland Glass Works").
—, October 1934, (Ruth Webb Lee, "The Tree of Life and Its Sundry Fruits").
—, April 1935, (Laura Watkins, "Positively Sandwich").

—, November 1936, (Laura Watkins, "Union Glass Co.").
—, May 1939, (Laura Watkins, "More Sandwich Patterns").

Hobbies, August 1938, ("Glassware Patents of Augustas Heisey").
—, January 1966.

Magazine of Old Glass, July 1938.

National Antiques Review, June 1971.

National Early American Glass Club Bulletin, June 1962; Winter 1986-87.

Books
Swan, Frank H. *Portland Glass Company.* Providence, RI: Roger Williams Press, 1939.
—, *Portland Glass.* Providence, RI: Roger Williams Press, 1949.
—, rev. and enlarged by Marion Dana. *Portland Glass.* Des Moines, IA: Wallace-Homestead Book Co., n.d.

Other Sources
Dana, Marion. Letters to authors, February 12, 1977 and August 16, 1977.

Farley, C.H. Letter, November 20, 1950. Collection of Maine Historical Society.

Portland Advertiser, November 1863.

Portland Business Directory, 1866-69, 1871-73.

Portland Board of Trade Journal, May 1888.

Portland City Directory, 1866-73.

Webb's N. E. Railway & Manufactures Statistical Gazetteer.

Glass and Glassmaking
General References
Barret, Richard Carter. *A Collector's Handbook of Blown and Pressed American Glass.* Manchester, VT: Forward's Color Productions, Inc., 1966.

Barrington-Haynes, E. *Glass Through the Ages.* London, 1959.

Belknap, G. McCanby, *Milk Glass.* NY: Crown Publishers, 1949.

Berlye, M.K. *The Encyclopedia of Working with Glass.* n.p.: Everest House, 1983.

Charleston, R.J. *Masterpiece of Glass: A World History from Corning Museum of Glass.* Corning, NY: Corning Museum, 1980.

Drahotova, Olga. *European Glass.* NY: Excalibur Books, 1983.

Dreppard, Carl W. *ABC's of Old Glass.* NY: Awards Books, 1966.

Graham, B. *Engraving Glass.* NY: Van Nostrand Reinhold, 1982.

Grow, Lawrence. *The Warner Collector's Guide to Pressed Glass.* NY Warner Books, 1982.

Heacock, William. *Encyclopedia of Victorian Colored Pattern Glass.* n.p.: Antique Publishers, 1967.
—, *Old Pattern Glass.* n.p.: Antique Publishers, 1981.
—, *Collecting Glass*, vol. 3. n.p.: Antique Publishers, 1986.

Honey, W. *Glass.* London: Victoria and Albert Museum, 1946.

Kamm, Minnie Watson. *Pattern Glass*, 8 vols. Grosse Point, MI: Kamm Publishers, 1939-54.
—, *Two Hundred Pattern Glass Pitchers.* Grosse Point, MI: Kamm Publishers, 1968.

Knittle, R.M. *Early American Glass.* NY: Appleton Century, 1937.

Lee, Ruth Webb. *Handbook of Early American Pressed Glass Patterns.* Wellesley Hills, MA: Lee Publications, 1936.
—, *Sandwich Glass:* The History of the Boston and Sandwich. Wellesley Hills, MA: Lee Publication, 1939.
—, *Victorian Glass.* Wellesley Hills, MA: Lee Publication, 1940.
—, *Antiques Fakes and Reproductions.* Wellesley Hills, MA: Lee Publication, 1950.
—, *Early American Pressed Glass*, enlarged and rev.ed. Wellesley Hills, MA: Lee Publication 1960.

Lewis, J.S. *Old Glass and How to Collect It.* Philadelphia: Lippincott, n.d.

Macifer, Percival. *The Glass Collector.* NY Dodd, Mead Co., 1919.

Matcham, J. *The Techniques of Glass Engraving.* NY: Larousse & Co., 1982.

McKearin, George S., and Helen. *American Glass.* NY: Crown Publishers, 1941.

Metz, Alice Hulett. *Early American Pattern Glass.* Beverton, OR: Charles Metz, 1958.
—*Much More Early American Pattern Glass.* Beverton, OR: Charles Metz. 1965.

Middlemes, Keith. *Antique Glass in Color.* NY: Doubleday, 1971.

Millard, S.T. *Goblets.* Topeka, KS: S.T. Millard, 1938.
—, *Goblets*, second ed. Topeka, KS: S.T. Millard, 1940.

Newman, H. *An Illustrated Dictionary of Glass.* London: n.p., 1977.

Northend, M. *American Glass.* NY: Dodd, Mead, 1926.

Papert, Emma. *Illustrated Guide to American Glass.* NY: Hawthorne Books, (date?)

Polak, A. *Glass: Its Makers and Its Public.* London: n.p., 1975.

Rivi, Albert Christian. *American Pressed Glass and Figure Bottles.* NY: Thomas Nelson, Inc., 1964.
—*American Cut and Engraved Glass.* NY: Thomas Nelson. Inc., 1965.
—*19th Century Glass: Its Genesis and Development,* NY: Thomas Nelson, Inc.,1967.

Roscoe, H.E., and C. Schorlemmer, *Treatise on Chemistry*, vol. 2. London: Macmillan & Co., 1913.

Savage, G. *Glass of the World.* n.p.: Galahad Books. 1975.

Schwartz, Marvin D. *Collector's Guide to Antique American Glass.* NY: Doubleday, 1969.

Spillman, Jane S. *American and European Pressed Glass in the Corning Museum of Glass.* Corning, NY: Corning Museum, n.d.

Thuro, Catherine M.V. *Oil Lamps*: *The Kerosene Era in North America*. Des Moines, IA: Wallace Homestead Book Co., 1976.

Van Tassel, Valentine. *American Glass*. NY: Chanticleer Press, 1950.

Walker, Elizabeth, and John Walker. *Pressed Glass in America: The First Hundred Years, 1825-1925*. n.p.: Antique Acres, 1986.

Wilson, Kenneth. *New England Glass and Glassmaking*. NY: Thomas Y. Crowell Co., 1972.

Other References

Brownell, Charles DeWolf. *Indian Races of North and South America*. NY: American Subscription House. 1857.

Emery, George Alex. *Ancient City or Gorgeana and Modern Town of York*. York, ME: York Corner Courier Steam Job Print, 1894.

Herber, Richard. *Modern Maine*, vol. 2. NY: Lewis Historical Publishing Co., 1971.

Moulton, Augustas F. *Portland by the Sea* Augusta, ME: Katahdin Publishing Co., 1926.

Reiley, Robin. *Wedgwood Jasper*. NY: World Publishing Co. 1972.

Willis, William. *History of Portland*. n.p.: Roger Williams Press, 1939.

Index

Note: Pages in ( ) indicate illustrations. Underline indicates primary entry.

Value Guide

Page 50
Cut Overlay chalice $1,200.00

Page 51
Tree of Life Hand compote clear $75.00-85.00
    sapphire blue $500.00-600.00
    apple green $1,000.00
    red or vinaceous purple $2,000.00

Page 52
Tree of Life with Sprig covered
    Sugar chestnut finial $175.00-195.00
    Tree of Life finial with clear band $85.00
Tree of Life with Sprig water pitcher . $300.00-350.00

Page 53
Tree of Life three pc set in silver holders
    signed Webster $2,000.00

Page 54
Tree of Life Hand compote
Pequot Sauce in sapphire blue $250.00
    clear $45.00

Page 55
Tree of Life finger bowls (sometimes called waste
    bowls) clear $15.00-20.00
    amber $75.00
    light blue $95.00
    cobalt $110.00
    apple green $145.00
    red $500.00
Small leaf shaped sauce clear $15.00
    amber $45.00
    red $300.00
    canary yellow $100.00
    other colors $45.00-100.00
Lemonade signed P.G. Co. Patent $125.00
    unsigned $75.00
Goblet signed P.G. Co. Patent $100.00
    unsigned $50.00

Page 56
Tree of Life, Handled Wine; clear $35.00-45.00
    Purple $750.00
Large leaf-shaped sauce clear $18.00-20.00
    Ice cream tray clear $65.00
    canary $500.00
    amber $100.00
    red $1,200.00

Page 57
Child Samuel compote clear $1,000.00
    canary yellow $2,000.00
    vaseline $1,500.00
    apple green $2,500.00

Page 59
Tree of Life shell bowl $145.00
    shell platter $195.00

Page 60
Tree of Life Peacock Blue Sweet Meat
    in silver holder $195.00
Tree of Life creamer in silver holder signed
    J. Babcock $125.00
Small Epergne with hand $250.00

Page 61
Tree of Life large single epergne $175.00-200.00
Leaf Sauces $45.00-500.00
Sugar signed P.G. Co. Patent $195.00

Page 62
Tree of Life Stained Glass Window .... N.A.

Page 64
Ophidian Epergne with double red snakes . $1,800.00
    green $1,500.00
    two color $1,600.00

Page 65
Ophidian compote colored snakes .. $500.00-900.00
    goblets with snakes $250.00
    without $65.00
    colored $125.00
    Handled wine $65.00
Ophidian Scalloped edge bowl clear $85.00
    raspberry $500.00

Page 66
Ophidian Vase with green snake $800.00
Finger Bowl clear $35.00
    chartreuse $150.00
Nautilus Shell in branches $100.00
    signed $300.00

Page 67
Condiment server $85.00-100.00
Wine set with enameled green
    decanter, six wines $950.00

Page 68
Handled Wine $65.00
Leaf dish clear $75.00
    raspberry $425.00
Ophidian Fruit sugar in green w/gold $850.00
Crackle Tankard $250.00
Crackle square dish in pewter holder red .. $350.00

Page 69
Crackle bud vase in silver holder ... $100.00-125.00
Leaf relish $45.00
Small compote $95.00
Footed Wines $45.00

Page 70
Lotus shallow oval bowl $45.00

Page 71
Lotus bread tray $85.00
Garden of Eden mug .... N.A.

Page 72
Garden of Eden goblet $175.00

Page 73
Tree of Life Milk Glass pickle caster $95.00
Covered Sugar $75.00
    enameled multicolor $275.00-300.00
Cruet $110.00
Salt blue $150.00
    white $95.00
    enameled multicolor $195.00
Covered Biscuit Jar $375.00
Straight sided berry bowl enameled $275.00
    plain $125.00

Sauce Dishes enameled $150.00
Page 74
Tree of Life Milk Glass free form berry bowl.$295.00
Horsehead Medallion Celery $85.00
Page 75
Ophidian bowl with applied feet $225.00
Page 76
Ophidian compote....................................$650.00
Page 77
Owl and Possum goblet.................$100.00-110.00
Page 78
Squirrel pitcher..........................$135.00-150.00
Page 79
Squirrel Footed berry bowl $145.00
Page 80
Deer and Pine water pitcher $125.00
Goblet... $85.00
Page 81
Rose Band Water set six tumblers.............$275.00
Rose Band butter dish $165.00
Page 82
Open Sugar $65.00
    covered $110.00
Vase small $550.00
    medium $65.00
    large...$95.00
    giant $250.00
Dahlia mug clear $35.00
    color..$85.00-100.00
Page 83
Pot de creme clear...................................$95.00
    green...$175.00
Sauce dish clear $15.00
    colored......................................$35.00-45.00
Dahlia covered sugar $55.00
Page 84
Double Egg Cup.......................................$75.00
Dirigo Pear relish $85.00
Dirigo Pear relish $95.00
Page 85
Dirigo Pear sauce small.............................$25.00
    large...$30.00
Birch Leaf large clear $35.00
    colored..$95.00
    small clear $15.00
    color..$35.00
Page 86
Oak Leaf Band goblet
    with prisms..$55.00
Oak Leaf Medallion goblet $45.00
Page 87
Acorn Band low compote flint.........$95.00-110.00
Page 88
Acorn Band milk pitcher flint....................$135.00
Gentleman's goblet $45.00
Irregular band goblet $45.00
Page 89
Feather emerald green pitcher..................$145.00

Page 90
Loop and Jewel butter................................$55.00
Loop and Heart lamp $85.00
Page 91
Loop and Jewel covered high
    standard compote $195.00
Page 93
Loop and Jewel Hand lamp $110.00
Loop and Jewel goblet...............................$45.00
Page 94
Festoon marmalade $85.00
Plate $110.00
Page 95
Festoon compote......................................$65.00
Pequot footed sauce sapphire blue $225.00
Page 96
Pequot Open compote $85.00
Covered compote.....................................$185.00
Goblet amber $175.00
Page 97
Fine Cut and Block sauce colored blocks........$45.00
Page 98
Fine Cut and Block Diamond Block
Egg cup $45.00
Marmalade $75.00
Covered sugar..$65.00
Creamer...$35.00
Jelly compote $25.00
Small compote $35.00
Medium compote $45.00
Large compote $65.00
Gent's goblet..$45.00
Lady's goblet..$35.00
Champagne $55.00
Water pitcher..$55.00
Milk pitcher $45.00
Large sauce $18.00
Small sauce $15.00
Fan dish $45.00
Small punch bowl $85.00
Tumbler...$18.00
Spooner $35.00
Punch cups $20.00
Berry bowl $35.00
Butter dish $75.00-80.00
Finger bowl..$25.00
Open salt $25.00
Salt shaker $25.00
Cake Stand..................................$40.00-45.00

Fine Cut and Block comes in more colors than any other pattern. For amber add 75%, for aquamarine add 100%, for sapphire blue add 125%, for yellow blocks add 80%, for pink blocks add 85%, for blue blocks add 125%, for green or orange blocks add 150%, for color flashing on colored glass add 300%, all other colors are rare enough so that no price can be set.

Tumbler..$50.00
Butter...$125.00
Sugar..$95.00
Creamer..$75.00
Toothpick $60.00

Page 137

Francisware child's pitcher $125.00
Syrup $160.00

Page 138

Clear bowl $65.00
Magnet and Grape flint goblet shield..........$95.00
Spooner..$85.00

Page 139

Frosted Leaf flint butter $150.00

Page 140

Master salt...$85.00
Double Egg cup $125.00
Lady's goblet..$95.00
Gentleman's goblet $110.00

Page 141

Quart decanter $250.00
Lady's goblet..$95.00

Page 142

Greek Key goblet flint.................................$65.00
Decanter..$145.00

Page 143

Etched Fern water bottle.............................$75.00
Cumberland goblet $15.00-20.00

Page 144

Broken Column covered small
    compote red flashes...........................$350.00

Page 145

Portland Souvenir Sauce dish
    hand decorated $95.00
Basket $150.00

Page 146

Candlestick................................$150.00-175.00
Lamp $95.00
Punch bowl..$150.00
Punch cups $15.00-20.00

Page 147

Cruet $75.00
Salt shaker $20.00
Toothpick $25.00
Syrup $75.00
Relish in silver holder $35.00
Atomizer...$65.00

Page 148

Banded Portland goblet...............................$45.00

Page 149

Berry bowl ruby flashed $500.00
    clear...$45.00
Banded Portland vase flashed yellow..........$45.00
Cider pitcher maiden's blush $275.00
    clear...$95.00
Pin tray red..$75.00

Page 150

Perfume bottles color flashed $75.00
    clear...$20.00

Salt maiden's blush $45.00
Covered jelly compote $85.00

Page 151

Butter gold flashed...................................$125.00

Page 152

O'Hara pitcher $55.00
Compote $45.00
Goblet...$35.00

Page 153

Prism flint compote....................................$25.00
Scalloped flute compote ....$135.00+
    Not enough sales to establish a price.

Page 155

Nestor tumbler clear $15.00
    amethyst..$45.00

Page 156

Honeycomb butter $65.00
Covered oval dish..$85.00

Page 157

Honeycomb creamer $25.00
Broken Column sugar red flashed............$150.00
    clear...$45.00
Creamer red flashed.................................$135.00
    clear...$45.00

Page 158

Broken Column punch cup cobalt $150.00
    clear...$25.00

Page 159

Falmouth goblet...$30.00

Page 160

Snow Drop shell sauce...............................$15.00
Snow Drop goblet..$35.00
Egg in Snow plate $20.00

Page 161

Orbed Feet mustard.....................................$35.00
Orbed Feet toothpick $25.00
Orbed Feet salt $15.00
Orbed Feet creamer $15.00-20.00
Orbed Feet goblet..$45.00
Bar Glass $50.00-150.00

Page 162

Casco goblet $15.00-20.00

Page 163

Tree of Life Child Samuel
cake stand $1,000.00

Page 165

Cut Fern creamer with reeded handle $65.00

Page 170

Broken Column Carafe clear $75.00
    red flashed $250.00

Page 172

Garden of Eden pitcher............................$185.00

Page 174

Roman Rosette creamer clear....................$30.00
    red flashed $95.00

N.A.—Price Not Avaiable.

Schroeder's Antiques Price Guide

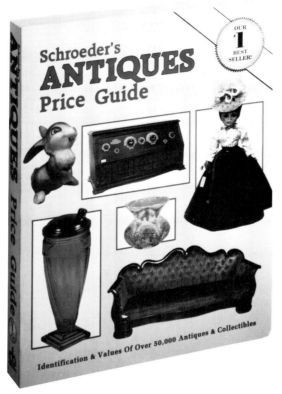

Schroeder's Antiques Price Guide has become THE household name in the antiques and collectibles field. Our team of editors works year-round with more than 200 contributors to bring you our #1 best-selling book on antiques and collectibles.

With more than 50,000 items identified and priced, Schroeder's is a must for the collector & dealer alike. If it merits the interest of today's collector, you'll find it in Schroeder's. Each subject is represented with histories and background information. In addition, hundreds of sharp original photos are used each year to illustrate not only the rare and unusual, but the everyday "fun-type" collectibles as well — not postage stamp pictures, but large close-up shots that show important details clearly.

Our editors compile a new book each year. Never do we merely change prices. Accuracy is our primary aim. Prices are gathered over the entire year previous to publication, from ads and personal contacts. Then each category is thoroughly checked to spot inconsistencies, listings that may not be entirely reflective of actual market dealings, and lines too vague to be of merit. Only the best of the lot remains for publication. You'll find Schroeder's Antiques Price Guide the one to buy for factual information and quality.

No dealer, collector or investor can afford not to own this book. It is available from your favorite bookseller or antiques dealer at the low price of $12.95. If you are unable to find this price guide in your area, it's available from Collector Books, P.O. Box 3009, Paducah, KY 42002-3009 at $12.95 plus $2.00 for postage and handling. 8½ x 11", 608 Pages $12.95

COLLECTOR BOOKS

A Division of Schroeder Publishing Co., Inc.